LITTLE BOOK OF BRAY AND ENNISKERRY

BRIAN WHITE

The History Press Ireland

First published 2016
This edition published 2018

The History Press Ireland
50 City Quay
Dublin 2
Ireland
www.thehistorypress.ie

The History Press Ireland is a member of Publishing Ireland,
the Irish book publishers' association.

British Library Cataloguing in Publication Data.
A catalogue record for this book is available from the British Library.

ISBN 978 0 7509 8791 2

Typesetting and origination by The History Press
Printed and bound by TJ International Ltd, Padstow, Cornwall

CONTENTS

1.	Geography and History	5
2.	Fact, Myth and Legend	17
3.	Famous Faces	35
4.	Mansions, Houses and Hotels	53
5.	Churches and Schools	75
6.	Work	91
7.	Bridges, Streets and Monuments	99
8.	Transport and Communications	107
9.	Sports and Entertainment	123
10.	Youth	129
11.	Law and Mayhem	131
12.	Wildlife	139

1

GEOGRAPHY
AND HISTORY

The development of Bray was overseen by Lord Meath, and the development of Enniskerry was carefully planned by Lord Powerscourt. Both lords were granted their properties in the 1600s.

The coming of the railway to Bray in 1854 divides the old era from the modern era of the town. Prior to 1854, Bray was only a small fishing village. It was granted township status in 1866, and following the Public Health Act of 1875 the death rate fell and the town became one of the healthiest towns in Ireland. Victorians were encouraged to leave the city smog and take the sea breezes at Blackrock, Kingstown and Bray. The town council provided musical events on the Esplanade and the railway company provided bathing boxes. The hotels and boarding houses offered mainly Scottish, Welsh, English and Northern Irish visitors '*A Céad Mile Fáilte*' ('100,000 welcomes'). Each grouping had set weeks

that they came, from May to the end of August. The population of the town doubled during the summer months. Bray soon won the title of the 'Irish Brighton'. Commerce was driven by the railway, with many shops refunding railway fare if a patron spent more than £2.

Aside from tourism, the printing trade was the mainstay of the town until the Solus Teo lamp factory was opened in 1935. The next wave of development came in the 1950s, with the opening of Industrial Yarns and Ardmore Studio. The town prospered between the end of the Second World War and the mid-1960s when the British tourists started taking charter flights to the Spanish resorts.

Bray fortunes declined and it eventually became a commuter hub for Dublin. In 1984 the railway line between Dublin and Bray was electrified and the service is now called the DART (Dublin Area Rapid Transport).

BRAY

Bray is a coastal town 20km south of Dublin. It is the largest town in County Wicklow. The town of Bray is the ninth largest urban area in Ireland, with a population of 31,872 as per the 2011 census. The area has four limits:

(1) Bray Civil Parish
(2) The Bray Township area
(3) The Municipal District
(4) Bray Postal Area

The Bray Civil Parish is an area in the centre of the town covering 425 acres.

The chief inhabitants of Bray, using the Town Improvements (Ireland) Act of 1854, incorporated themselves into a governing body on 9 October 1857. Bray was granted township status on 23 July 1866 and included the following townlands: Bray Civil Parish, Little Bray, Ravenswell, Killarney, Kilbride, Oldcourt, Ballwaltrim, Springfield, Ballymorris, Newcourt and part of Old Connaught.

Bray Municipal District was incorporated in 2014 and comprises all the townlands in Bray Township, Enniskerry, Kilmacanogue and Powerscourt.

The Bray Postal area begins one mile south of Shankill County Dublin and extends southwards to Glendalough. The West boundary is Kippure Mountain and the border to the east is the Irish Sea. Towns included are Bray, Enniskerry, Roundwood, Laragh, Kilcoole, Greystones and Newtownmountkennedy.

ENNISKERRY

Enniskerry is a townland in the Parish of Powerscourt. The village of Enniskerry is made up of three townlands: Cookstown, Knocksink, and the townland of Enniskerry. Both Bray and Enniskerry are in the half-barony of Rathdown.

The whole of Enniskerry has developed under the guidance of the Wingfield family, and the area has remained an agricultural area mainly consisting of small farm holdings. Forestry has long played a vital role in the Glencree Valley.

POWERSCOURT TOWNLANDS

The spelling of the Powerscourt townlands has changed over the past 400 years. Mervyn Wingfield, the 7th Lord Powerscourt, listed the changes in 1903 in his book, *A Description of Powerscourt.*

Old Name	Modern Name
Beanaghbegg (Little Beanagh) Beanaghmore (Great Beanagh)	Bahana
Oenagh or Ownagh	Onagh
Kiltagaran	Kilgarron
Cookeston	Cookstown
Annacrew or Ballycale or Aghnacrevy	Annacrevy
Ballycortell or Cortellstown	Curtlestown
Barnemoyre or Barnameare	Barnamire
Ballybrowe	Ballybrew
Killeger	Killegar
Classganny	Glaskenny
Manister	Monastry
Lackindarragh	Lackandarragh
Bolreagh	Ballyreagh
La Croine or Croane	Crone
Ballynegeeogh	Ballinagee
Ballinacahill	Ballycoyle

The Park	Deerpark or The Paddock
Aghnaggare	Aurora
Corbollyes	Old Boleys
Glancree or Glencry	Glencree
Ballynornan or Ballyornane	Ballyornan

BRAY TIMELINE

Year	Event
1173	Richard de Clare, Earl of Pembroke, granted Bray Manor to Walter de Riddlesford.
1225	'The Song of Dermot and the Earl', lines 3092-3095, makes reference to Bray and County Wicklow.
1335	Goffery Cramp was given lands at the Manor of Oldcourt, Bray, County Wicklow.
1402	John Drake, Mayor of Dublin, led British forces in a skirmish against the Wicklow clans at Sunnybank, Bray, known as the Battle of Bloody Bank.
1428	The Viceroy mustered a force of Dublin men at Bray, and led an attack on the O'Byrne Clan.
1535	Fassaroe Castle near Bray was built for Sir William Brabazon, Vice Treasurer and General Receiver of Ireland.
1609	St Paul's church, Bray, built.
1618	Killruddery Estate, Bray, was granted to Sir William Brabazon.
1657	Work began on the first Bray Bridge over the Dargle River.
1659	Population of Bray reaches 300.
1666	The first Bray Bridge completed.
1666	The lands at Oldcourt, Bray, are granted to the Edwards family.
1666	Earliest record of births in Church of Ireland parish of Bray.
1666	Earliest record of marriage in Church of Ireland parish of Bray.

1666	Earliest record of deaths in Church of Ireland parish of Bray.
1692	Bray barracks are built.
1741	Bray Bridge was carried away in a storm.
1762	Bray Town Pound House was erected near the site of the present Town Hall.
1770	St Paul's church was extended and repaired.
1776	Qunis Coaching Inn (now Royal Hotel) was established in Bray.
1804	Three Martello Towers were built in Bray (1) Southern end of Bray Prom (2) near the Harbour (3) Corke Abbey. Each cost £1,800.
1813	Sir Philip Crampton was granted Lough Bray by Lord Powescourt.
1818	The Earl of Meath purchased the Baracks of Bray for a Fever Hospital for £100.
1821	The population of Bray stands at 2,029, or 1.8 per cent of county population.
1831	The population of Bray stands at 3,758 or 3.09 per cent of county population.
1833	An outbreak of cholera in Bray kills twenty-five people.
1834	The Conservatory was erected by the Putland family at San Souci (now Loreto Convent, Bray).
1837	A police station was built for the RIC near the Royal Hotel, Bray.
1841	The population of Bray stands at 3,169, or 2.51 per cent of county population.
1846	An act was obtained to extend the Dublin & Kingstown Line to Bray Bridge.
1847	Work began on laying the railway tracks around Bray Head. 500 men undertook the work.
1850	The first Mass was celebrated in the Loreto Convent, Bray, and Mother Conception Lopez, a native of Spain, was appointed Mother Superior of the convent.
1850	The Holy Redeemer church, Bray, was enlarged by the addition of 33ft to the nave and a tower was erected.

1851	The population of Bray stands at 3,156, or 3.18 per cent of county population.
1854	The first train left Bray Railway Station.
1856	A new Bray Bridge over the Dargle River was designed by David Edge.
1857	The Church of Ireland at Kilbride, Bray, was built.
1861	The foundation stone for Christ Church, Bray was laid.
1861	The population of Bray was 4,182, or 4.8 per cent of county population.
1862	Aravon School, Bray, was founded.
1862	Carlisle Sports Grounds, Quinsborough Road, Bray was opened by the Lord Lieutenant of Ireland, Lord Carlisle.
1864	St Andrew's Methodist church, Florence Road, Bray was built.
1864	French School, Bray, was founded by Madame de Mailly.
1866	Bray Township Act was passed.
1871	The population of Bray stands at 6,087, or 7.73 per cent of county population.
1877	The first meeting of the Girls' Friendly Society of Ireland took place in Bray.
1881	Bray Township Act raised funds for the building of a sea wall.
1881	Work began on building the Town Hall and Market Place, Bray. The site was donated by the Earl of Meath.
1885	Bray Emmets GAA Club was established.
1886	Bray & Enniskerry Light Railway Company Act was passed.
1890	An act was obtained to construct at harbour at Bray, at the cost of £45,000.
1891	The population of Bray stands at 6,888 or 11.08 per cent of county population.
1891	Bray Electricity Light Company was established at the Mill Race, Bray.
1894	County Wicklow Lawn Tennis Club, Bray, was established.
1896	Bray Sailing Club was founded.

1897	Bray Golf Club was formed.
1901	The Sisters of Charity was establish Ravenswell School, Little Bray.
1901	The population of Bray stands at 7,424, or 12.20 per cent of county population.
1904	The Post Office on the Quinsboro Road, Bray, was built.
1911	The population of Bray stands at 7,691, or 12.66 per cent of county population.
1911	Cearbhall O'Dalaigh was born at 85 Main Street, Bray. In 1974 he became fifth President of Ireland.
1911	Bray Public Library was built on Florence Road at a cost of £2,000.
1922	Bray Wanderer's Football Club was originally established.
1925	The Bray Urban District Council vote to drop the name Bri Cualann and revert to that of Bray.
1926	The population of Bray stands at 8,637, or 14.99 per cent of county population.
1931	Bray Technical School was the first new school approved under the 1930 Vocational Education Act.
1935	Building of kiosks on Bray seafront began.
1936	The population of Bray stands at 10,111, or 17.26 per cent of county population.
1950	Holy Year Cross was erected on Bray Head and dedicated.
1956	The population of Bray Urban District stands at 10,856, or 17.3 per cent of county population.
1957	The Lighthouse at Bray Harbour fell into the sea following a storm.
1958	Minister of Industry & Commerce, Seán Lemass, opened Ardmore Film Studio, Bray.
1961	The population of Bray Urban District stands at 11,856, or 19.8 per cent of county population.
1962	Arcadia Ballroom, Bray, was destroyed by fire.
1976	The chairlift on Bray Head ran commercially for the last time in 1976. The fittings were removed from 1977.

1979	The population of Bray Urban District stands at 21,773, or 25.9 per cent of county population.
1988	Gary O'Toole of Bray represented Ireland in swimming at the 1988 Olympic Games held in Seoul.
1996	The population of Bray Urban District stands at 25,252, or 24.6 per cent of county population.
1997	Disc Parking was introduced in Bray.
2001	The foundation stone of Bray Civic Centre unveiled by Taoiseach Bertie Ahern.
2012	Katie Taylor wins Gold for boxing at the Olympics in London.

ENNISKERRY TIMELINE

1603	Powerscourt, Enniskerry, County Wicklow was granted to Sir Richard Wingfield by King James I of England.
1715	The Powerscourt Arms Hotel, Enniskerry, was built.
1730	Work began on the building of Powerscourt House, Enniskerry.
1739	A road bridge at Enniskerry was destroyed in a storm.
1743	Powerscourt House, Enniskerry was completed.
1782	Henry Grattan purchased Tinnehinch Coaching Inn near Enniskerry. He did not take up residence until 1784.
1792	Charleville House, Enniskerry, was destroyed by fire.
1810	Charleville House (present house), Enniskerry, was built.
1818	Powerscourt National School, Enniskerry, was built.
1820	Henry Grattan, an MP who lived in Enniskerry, died in London and was buried in Westminster Abbey, London.
1820	Charleville House, Enniskerry rebuilt after the house was destroyed by fire in 1792.
1825	Earliest record of births in the Roman Catholic parish of Enniskerry.
1825	Earliest record of marriage in the Roman Catholic parish of Enniskerry.

1830	Between 1830 and 1845 Baroness Carolina Nairne lived in Enniskerry.
1841	The population of Enniskerry urban area stands at 448, or 0.36 per cent of county population.
1843	The Fountain and Town Clock at Enniskerry was erected by Lord Powerscourt to mark the 100-year anniversary of Powerscourt House.
1851	The population of Enniskerry urban area stands at 380, or 0.39 per cent of county population.
1855	The Forge and Blacksmith's House, Enniskerry, were built. The Forge cost £150, while the house cost £200.
1856	The Lower Road from Bray to Enniskerry was completed. Pre-1856 it led along the Back Dargle, via Powerscourt Gates to the village.
1859	St Patrick's church, Enniskerry, was built.
1859	St Mary's parish, Enniskerry, was constituted by Cardinal Cullen.
1860	The dome, designed by Sir George Moyers, was added to the Clock Tower in Enniskerry.
1861	The population of Enniskerry urban area stands at 374, or 0.43 per cent of county population.
1863	St Patrick's church, Enniskerry, officially opened.
1865	The spire was added to St Patrick's church, Enniskerry.
1871	The population of Enniskerry urban area stands at 381, or 0.48 per cent of county population.
1881	The population of Enniskerry urban area stands at 324, or 0.46 per cent of county population.
1886	The first attempt to link Bray and Enniskerry by railway was the establishment of the Bray & Enniskerry Light Railway Company.
1886	Bray & Enniskerry Light Railway Company Act was passed.
1891	The population of Enniskerry urban area stands at 256, or 0.41 per cent of county population.
1894	Powerscourt Arms Hotel, Enniskerry, was destroyed by fire.

1911	Enniskerry Public Library was built at Church Road, Enniskerry.
1924	The Wicklow Hills Bus Company established, based in the yard behind the Powerscourt Arms Hotel, Enniskerry.
1925	The Glencree river was damed near Enniskerry and a pumping station provided electricity for the village.
1926	The population of Enniskerry urban area stands at 214, or 0.37 per cent of county population.
1930	Lord Powerscourt laid the foundation stone for the Parish Hall, formerly the British Legion Hall, Bray Road, Enniskerry.
1936	The population of Enniskerry urban area stands at 145, or 0.24 per cent of county population.
1943	The film, *Henry IV*, starring Sir Lawrence Oliver, was shot at Powerscourt Estate, Enniskerry.
1956	The population of Enniskerry urban area stands at 530, or 0.88 per cent of county population.
1956	St Mary's GAA Club, Enniskerry established.
1958	Paul Henry, RHA, died at his home in Bray and was buried in St Patrick's graveyard, Enniskerry.
1961	The population of Enniskerry urban area stands at 652, or 1.11 per cent of county population.
1964	Charlie Keegan from Enniskerry won the World Ploughing Championship in Austria.
1965	The All-Ireland Ploughing Championships was held at Enniskerry on 17 and 18 November.
1971	Population of Enniskerry urban area 789, or 1.3 per cent of county population.
1974	Powerscourt House, Enniskerry, was destroyed by fire.
1979	The population of Enniskerry urban area stands at 1,185, or 1.4 per cent of county population.
1980	Frederick Forsyth (author) sold his home Kilgarron House, Enniskerry.
1981	St Mary's GAA Club, Enniskerry, opened Parc na Sillogue Enniskerry on land donated by Frederick Forsyth (author).

1985	Kilmacanogue parish church became a chapel of ease of Enniskerry parish church, St Mary's.
1996	The population of Enniskerry urban area stands at 2,118, or 2.06 per cent of county population.
1996	Powerscourt Golf Club (Enniskerry) was established.
2002	The population of Enniskerry urban area stands at 2,804, or 1.84 per cent of the county population.
2003	Charlie Keegan of Enniskerry died.

2

FACT, MYTH
AND LEGEND

THE GHOST OF BALLYORNEY

A number of people have reported seeing a ghostly carriage pulled by eight white horses and a driver sitting on the carriage, on the road between Powerscourt and the Waterfall gate. No one can explain why dogs, cats, sheep and cows cry out at 10.30 p.m. and an eerie feeling is cast over the area. Some local residents believe it is the livestock reacting to this ghostly figure. There have been a number of unexplained accidents involving horses on the banks of the Dargle River (see Lucky Escape, p. 20).

AWE AT THE WATERFALL

In 1777, Arthur Young, the first chairman of the English Board of Agriculture, visited the leafy and matchless green slopes of County Wicklow. At Powerscourt Waterfall, Young was struck with a sense of awe and pleasure. 'Romantic Glen,' he exclaimed, 'leaving scarce passage for the river at the bottom, which rages as with difficulty finding its way. It is the finest range of wood I have anywhere seen'.

MADAME TUSSAUD

In February 1805 Madame Tussaud came to Dublin with her son, Joseph, and their travelling exhibition. They stayed at 16 Clarendon Street in Dublin. She cast various models of Irish political figures during her visit, including the Right Hon. Henry Grattan from Enniskerry.

CUSTOMER COMPLAINT

In 1812 there was an irate customer who stayed at the Enniskerry Inn, a man by the name of William Smith. After his first night there he complained that a rat had gnawed the candle in his room, and that the rat had also chewed his shoes. There is no record of how the complaint was dealt with, but, needless to say, William Smith only spent one night in the inn.

WATERFALL DINNERS, 1827

Countess Monck, Lady Powerscourt and Revd Robert Daly, rector of Powerscourt Parish, inaugurated 'The Waterfall Dinners' in September 1827. The Waterfall Dinners had a twofold approach in their effort to support nine schools in the district of Bray and Enniskerry for both Roman Catholic and Protestants. Firstly, the ladies invited their friends from the district to a dinner in Powerscourt House. The invited ladies were asked to make a donation. They then enjoy the cooking of Lady Powerscourt and Lady Rathdowne. One of the main items on the menu was Lady Powerscourt's lemon cake.

In September 1827, the second approach consisted of taking some 530 children of the schools in the district by horse dray to Powerscourt Waterfall. Following games and novelty shows the children were taken across the rustic bridge at the waterfall where tables were laid out with roast beef, plum puddings, apple pie and feast of buns and cakes of all varieties. After a prize-giving for the sports competitions the children would be returned home. The memoirs of the Revd Robert Daly state that the Waterfall Dinners continued for three years up to 1830. This was the year that the National Education Act was passed, although free compulsory primary education was not introduced until 1870.

SCOTTISH BALLADS COMPOSED IN ENNISKERRY

The name of Caroline Olipant Baroness Narine is on a par with other Scottish writers, Sir Walter Scott, Robert Burns and James Hogg. But on the death of her husband, William Murray Narine, 5th Baron Nairne in 1830, Caroline left Gask in Scotland to settle in Enniskerry. She moved into a house on Church Hill, Enniskerry with her son, William the 6th

Baron Nairne. While in Enniskerry, from 1830 to 1834, she wrote the Jacobite ballads 'The Laird O'Cockpen', 'Charlie is my Darling', 'The Rowan Tree', 'The Auld House', and 'The Hundred Pipers'. Caroline used per pen name, Mrs Bogan of Bogan, or the simple version 'BB'. So the Scottish ballads were actually composed in Enniskerry. In 1834 she moved to Brussels, where her son died in 1837. She then returned to her native Scotland and died at Gask in 1845. She is buried in the family vault in the local graveyard.

BODY SNATCHING, 1833

The Murder Act of 1752 stipulated that only corpses of executed murders could be used for dissection. This left a shortfall for medical students, who had to prove their anatomical skills by dissecting a body. Grave robbers or 'sack 'em up men' saw a way to earn some money. It became normal practice that relatives of the deceased would stay at the graveside of the corpse for up to ten days after the burial. The Anatomy Act of 1832 licenced anatomy teachers to acquire corpses. A number of oversite commissioners were appointed to ensure the corpses did not come from grave robbers. In Bray, there is only one case of grave robbery. On 4 November 1833 the body of Lucy McKay was stolen from St Paul's graveyard. John McKay, the local schoolmaster, died upon hearing that his wife's body was stolen.

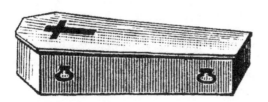

CLOCK TOWER, ENNISKERRY

The Clock Tower in Enniskerry was presented to the village of Enniskerry on St Patrick's Day 1843 by Richard, the 6th Lord Powerscourt. From the air the base of the clock tower makes the shape of a shamrock. The tower marks the centenary of the remodelling of Powerscourt House. The dome on the tower was added in 1860.

HALF-DAY FOR SCHOOL CHILDREN

On 16 October 1858, the Countess of Meath laid the foundation stone of the gas works at Bray harbour and the children of Bray had a half-day off school. This was the first time that school children in Ireland were given a half-day for a civic event. On 6 September 1858 Queen Victoria had preformed the official opening of Leeds Town Hall, and the children of Leeds were given a half-day off school. Lord Meath said, 'If the children of Leeds can get a half-day off school for a civic event, why should the children of Bray not get the same?'

The work on gas works was carried out by the engineer William Morley Stars of London to the specifications of the architect Edmund William O'Reilly.

LUCKY ESCAPE

In 1860 Lady Laura Grattan, the daughter-in-law of the patriot Henry Grattan, wanted to see the new road beside the Dargle River, made by Lord Monck. Feeling apprehension about this new road, which runs above a ravine at an elevation of 200ft, she had her phaeton prepare a carriage drawn by a single horse and driven by a faithful servant named Mr Gason. There had recently been heavy rains. At one point on the route Lady Grattan descended from the carriage, and suddenly the ground in front of the horse gave way. The carriage, horse and driver disappeared down a precipice of 150ft. The horse was killed, the carriage broke into pieces, but the driver walked away with just a deep cut to his forehead.

In honour of her escape, Lady Grattan donated a water fountain and two horse troughs to the city of Dublin. The fountain stands at the junction of Dawson's Street and St Stephens Green. A statue to her father-in-law, Henry Grattan, is in Dame Street.

ACT OF KINDNESS, DECEMBER 1878

Mrs Sutton, from Glencormac near Kilmacanogue, was crossing a gate on Bray Head when she got impaled. The son of Mrs Farrelly, who lived in a gate lodge on the Killruddery Estate on the slopes of Bray Head, came across Mrs Sutton. He managed to free her and take her back to the gate lodge.

Mrs Farrelly's daughter gave up her bed for Mrs Sutton, while the boy who had made the rescue was dispatched to Bray, to summon medical help. Dr Whistler and Dr Brigford came to the gate lodge at once. Lady Brabazon came to see Mrs Sutton and requested the doctors to send their medical bill to her. Mrs Sutton made a full recovery from her injuries.

MYSTERIOUS OUTRAGE, 1886

In an area called Annicerevy, about 2 miles west of Enniskerry, lived Mr Thomas Burton, his son John, and his daughter. On the night of 10 March 1886 Miss Burton was woken by the noise of her pony, which had got loose and was roaming around the farmyard. She woke her brother John, who hastily dressed. He went outside to discover that a rick of hay and stack of oats valued at £120 were in flames. Mr Burton and his son tried to extinguish the flames, but the hay and corn were reduced to ashes. Mr Burton set off in pursuit of the perpetrators. When he failed to return home his neighbours and the police constable mounted a search of the area but Mr Burton was never located.

AMERICAN SHAMROCK FUND TO HELP BRAY HOSPITALS

Over 206,000 Irishmen enlisted in the First World War. Men from Irish regiments made up 40 per cent of the strength of the British Army. The international Red Cross reported in August 1916 that the number of soldiers and sailors killed in action in the First World War was averaging 8,500 men per month and the seriously wounded were as many as 4,200. The military and public hospitals could not cope with the number of wounded soldiers and sailors returning to Ireland. A series of auxiliary hospitals were established and put under the care of the Red Cross and the St John's Ambulance Service. Two such hospitals were established in Bray, The Duke of Connaught and The Princess Patricia Hospital. These hospitals need specialised equipment because they were dealing with soldiers and sailors who had lost a limb.

The Duke of Connaught Hospital took over the Meath Industrial School for Girls. The school was located close to the Town Hall on the Vevay Road. The building is now St Patrick's National School. The Princess Patricia Hospital was located in the International Hotel beside Bray Railway Station.

There was a chronic need for funds and it was decided that a group of fundraisers should be sent to the United States. They had a poster designed by the famous designer Charles S. Jagger. The picture displayed a wounded soldier sitting on the ground being comforted by a woman under the Statue of Liberty, with the skyline of New York in the background. The banner on the poster read 'Eireann's Appeal to America "Help my Irish Soldiers"', and at the base of the poster the words 'Shamrock Fund' were written. The fundraising team was headed up by the Countess of Kingston, a relation of Lord Powerscourt, her niece Pearl Betram, secretary to the countess Mrs Mary Dougherty, and Harold Large from Dublin. They established offices at 39 East Street, New York. They enlisted the cream of American society to lend their names and support to the fundraising campaign, including the former president Teddy Roosevelt and the Revd Hanna.

They embarked on a three-year tour of America, not without problems. In New York they published a list of Irish soldiers wounded in the war, and included the pensions the soldiers were awarded. Immediately this was raised in the House of Commons as having a negative reaction on the morale of the soldiers serving in the theatre of war. The Countess Kingston made the counter argument that she had got American women to adopt a soldier in the trenches. The British Government asked the American newspapers not to publish details about any soldiers.

The next issue arose in a town called Spokane in Washington State, when the fundraisers were arrested for 'aggressive fundraising'. The town prosecutor gave them a 'get out of jail' card. If they called a hospital in Ireland after the town of Spokane they were free to go. You may ask what aggressive fundraising was; it meant that the party shipped out from Ireland real shamrocks and they sold them at $4 a sprig.

Another pair of fundraisers in the States at the time was Lord and Lady Aberdeen, who were collecting on behalf of Irish soldiers who had contracted TB in the trenches. Lord and Lady Aberdeen organised a concert in New York and the headline act was Charlie Chaplin. But Charlie went off to California to make a film and left Lord and Lady Aberdeen without a star performer. They had charged between $4 and 25c a seat. The prosecutor in New York was of the opinion that the Aberdeens failed in their commitment, and he withdrew their licence to raise funds, then gave Lord and Lady Aberdeen two weeks to leave the United Sates. In total, the Shamrock Fund raised $170,000 or £510,000 between 1916 and 1919. The two Bray hospitals treated over 5,400 wounded soldiers and sailors.

DOG RAGE IN BRAY AND THE PASTEUR INSTITUTE

On 27 January 1887 Patrick McEvoy, aged 2, from Little Bray, was bitten seven times on his head and limbs. The medical team thought the dog may have had rabies. It was decided that the best treatment was at the Pasteur Institute in Paris and Patrick was treated there between 5 February and 4 March 1887. Patrick made a full recovery.

THE FIRST SMOKING BAN

Smoking in the workplace in Ireland was banned on 29 March 2004. However, more than 100 years earlier the Town Clerk of Bray, Mr P.M. McDonnell gave evidence on 29 November 1888 to the Royal Commission on Market Rights and Tolls in Ireland, and he stated that under the Bray Township Acts 1881 and bylaw 185 'No person shall smoke tobacco or other like thing in the market-house, or any covered building connected therewith'. The report of Market Rights and Tolls was presented by the Commissioners, Charles Black and John J. O'Meara before both houses of parliament in 1891.

GREAT POTATO EXPERIMENT, 1891

Following the famine of 1845-1847 the Royal Dublin Society and the major estate owners in Ireland carried out a great potato experiment in 1891. The parameters of the experiment were drawn up by the Royal Dublin Society. The land owners were to use eighteen different varieties of seed potatoes. Farmyard dung was applied at the rate of twenty tons per acre.

The results of Lord Powerscourt's experiment:

No	Variety	Small	Diseased	Large	Total
1	Robertson's Victory	20lb 8oz	2lb 0oz	132lb 8oz	155lb 0oz
2	Scotch Champion	20lb 0oz	4lb 0oz	124lb 0oz	148lb 0oz

3	Farmer	21lb 4oz	12lb 4oz	108lb 8oz	142lb 0oz
4	White Rock	11lb 0oz	4lb 0oz	116lb 8oz	131lb 8oz
5	Union	4lb 0oz	5lb 0oz	121lb 8oz	130lb 8oz
6	Irish Champion	28lb 8oz	5lb 8oz	97lb 8oz	130lb 8oz
7	Imperator	14lb 12oz	4lb 0oz	106lb 8oz	125lb 4oz
8	Bruce	5lb 0oz	1lb 8oz	114lb 8oz	121lb 0oz
9	Colonel	20lb 12oz	5lb 4oz	93lb 0oz	119lb 0oz
10	American Earl Rose	9lb 8oz	9lb 8oz	90lb 8oz	109lb 8oz
11	Magnum Bonum	10lb 4oz	0lb 8oz	96lb 4oz	107lb 0oz
12	Reading Hero	8lb 8oz	1lb 8oz	97lb 8oz	104lb 0oz
13	Early White Rose	11lb 4oz	6lb 8oz	86lb 4oz	104lb 0oz
14	Puritan	9lb 12oz	5lb 0oz	84lb 12oz	99lb 8oz
15	Skerry Blue	17lb 0oz	2lb 0oz	79lb 8oz	93lb 8oz
16	Beauty of Hebron	11lb 4oz	6lb 0oz	74lb 4oz	91lb 8oz
17	Early Kemps	10lb 4oz	7lb 0oz	70lb 0oz	87lb 4oz
18	General	13lb 0oz	13lb 8oz	58lb 8oz	85lb 0oz

The best indicator for the price of potatoes in the famine period comes from the parliamentary reports from 1840 to 1846 for the market town of Bray, which shows the price of a stone-weight of potatoes for the week ending 24 January. Bray had the highest price in County Wicklow for potatoes in 1844 and 1846. The price difference in Bray for the years 1845 and 1846 showed an increase of 54.54 per cent in the price of potatoes.

Year	1840	1841	1842	1843	1844	1845	1846
Price per stone in pence	3½	3	2½	4	3	3	5½

WATER-DOWSING EXPERIMENT

In 1899 Sir William Fletcher Barrett, a professor of the Royal Academy of Science in Dublin, organised a water-dowsing experiment. He selected a number of fields near his home in Carrigoona, Bray. The first water dowser was Mr William Stone from Wiltshire in England. On arrival at Kingstown (now Dún Laoghaire) he was blindfolded and taken to Ardmore House (now Ardmore Film Studio), the home of Judge LeFroy. On 2 April 1899 Mr Stone was taken to the field, blindfolded, and he walked the field and indicated with his dowsing rods the location of water. These results were marked on a map of the field. The blindfold was removed and Mr Stone walked the field for a second time again, plotting the indications of water on the map. Mr Barrett got a second dowser, Mr J.H. Jones from Waterford. He was also blindfolded for his first attempt and the blindfold was removed for his second attempt. The four readings were carefully measured, and in some cases the indications of water by Mr Stone and Mr Jones were within inches of each other. To prove the existence of water in the field in July 1899 Mr Barrett sunk four wells. Water was found at depths less than 25ft below the surface in each of the four wells. The wells have never run dry and they are marked on OS Maps 6-inch Wicklow (Rathdown) Sheet VII.8.

Sir William Fletcher Barrett published the results of the water dowser experiment in 1910, in a publication entitled *The history and mystery of the so called divining or dowsing rod*. This publication is regarded as the best evidence of the success of water divining. Sir William Barrett set down five conditions and criteria for the experiment; (1) the place chosen for the experiment had to be entirely unfamiliar to the dowser, (2) the person accompanying the dowser had to be ignorant of the geology of the area, (3) the dowser had to be taken immediately to the site, without being able to talk to any local inhabitants, (4) no indications could be given to the dowser of the lie land (while blindfolded), and (5) all independent observers had to take notes and make a written report.

The observers included Mr Barrett, Mr Charles St George LeFroy, Mr J.A. Cunningham, and junior members of the Geological Society.

A LA POWERSCOURT

In 1902 cookbooks carried a new recipe called 'A La Powerscourt', devised at Powerscourt House, Enniskerry, County Wicklow. It consisted of slices of bread, toasted and buttered. They were then covered with minced sardines and finished with a poached egg laid on top of each, with a nice garnish of pickled beets.

EMPIRE DAY

On 22 May 1904 Lord Meath instituted Empire Day in the United Kingdom. The day was selected because it was the birthday of Queen Victoria, who had died in 1901. On this day flags were flown on public buildings. In schools, morning classes were devoted to reminding children of their heritage. School children were given a

half-day off school. Lord Meath put up a prize fund for an essay that showed the virtues of good citizenship. In the evening, towns and villages put on a pageant and there was a fireworks display. In 1958, the House of Commons voted to rename Empire Day, Commonwealth Day.

MILITARY BATTLES AROUND ENNISKERRY

For four days, starting on 15 July 1907, the villages of South Dublin and North Wicklow were the scene of hand-to-hand combat between two military teams; 'The Reds' and 'The Blues'. The Red team, under the command of Colonel McClintock, was made up of forces from the 48th Battery Field Artillery from Kildare, a horse division from Athlone and a company of Engineers. The Blue force came from the Curragh 14th Infantry Brigade. The Reds took up a position near Raven's Rock. The Blues started in Stepaside in County Dublin and within an hour the Reds had fallen back to Onagh about 2 miles from Enniskerry. The right flank of the Reds forced the Blues to take the hamlet of Enniskerry and from 6 p.m. to 10 p.m. both sides took part in hand-to-hand combat. Both teams encamped for the night. The following day, two new companies were introduced, the Cameron Highlanders and the Berkshire Regiment. The command headquarters was set up at Onagh. Lady Powerscourt visited the command camp and invited the officers to Powerscourt House. The weather was reported as extremely hot and this took its toll on the troops. The military were given the right to go wherever they wanted, much to the annoyance of some of the locals. The military exercise concluded on Thursday 18 July, and the troops returned to their barracks to be given the results of the exercise.

BELGIAN REFUGEES

In 17 October 1914 the first fifty-six Belgian Refugees arrived in Bray and the local committee gave them a warm welcome. They walked from the station to their new home on the Meath Road. The home was sponsored by the Loreto Schools in Ireland and Mauritius. The Irish students and alumni raised over £100, but the convent in Mauritius gave over £300 and a quantity of clothing that was shipped free of charge by the Union and Castle Shipping Line. The French School and the Loreto School in Bray gave free education and books to the children of the refugees. Mrs Breslin, the owner of International Hotel, gave a piece of ground on Adelaide Road to the local Belgian Refugee committee at a nominal rent of £1 per annum. The local committee then applied to the Master of the Rolls to allow the Belgian refugees to use one of their fields for growing vegetables. In December 1914 the American Red Cross organised a parcel of clothing and toys for each Belgian child in Bray.

In August 1915 Pierre Romain, a 5-year-old Belgian refugee, was knocked down by a vehicle on Bray Esplanade and he was taken to Loughlinstown Infirmary by ambulance. By 1916 the number of refugees in Bray had risen to sixty and they had a profit of £100 from growing the vegetables. The field where the vegetables were grown is now Fáilte Park, the home of Bray Bowling Club. Bray locals still refer to the plot of ground as the 'Belgian Field'.

DARING RESCUE

Mr John Archer of Bray Head, County Wicklow, was a sailor on board the SS *Ulster* in 1916, which was berthed at North Wall in Dublin. John saw a soldier from the Highland Regiment fall between the vessel and the quay wall. John carried out a daring rescue at great risk to himself. Subsequently, the captain of the SS *Ulster* received a cheque from the lieutenant colonel of the Highland Regiment on behalf of officers of the regiment, to be passed on to Mr Archer in recognition of his actions. The Bray Town Commissioner, James Archer was a brother of John Archer.

PLANNING A NEW GOVERNMENT IN ENNISKERRY

In August 1927 there were fears that a General Election would be called. On 11 August 1927, Mr Johnson, the leader of the Labour Party, held a secret meeting in the Powerscourt Arms Hotel in Enniskerry. Present at the meeting was William O'Brien and a trade union leader R.J.P. Mortished. They discussed the possible line-up of ministers in a new administration should the government suffer a vote of no confidence on 16 August 1927. The names on the list were discussed, and when the meeting finished the list was torn up and placed in the bin in the hotel. The men were observed leaving the hotel by an *Irish Times* editor John Edward Healy. The editor, knowing about the crises in the Dáil, found the torn paper in the bin and the next day his newspaper listed certain person who might be offered a cabinet post in a new administration.

When the vote of no confidence was taken on 16 August 1927 it ended in a tie (71: 71), then the Ceann Comhairle cast his vote with the government. The Dail was dissolved on 21 August 1927, and the general election was held on 15 September 1927.

MOUNT MAULIN HOTEL AND FUR FARM

Silver Fox and fur farm nestled in the 145 acres attached to Mount Maulin Hotel near Powerscourt Waterfall in the 1930s. The first litter of silver foxes was born at Mount Maulin in April 1933, and large litters of other animals were successfully reared during 1932 and 1933. Visitors to the hotel could visit the pens and ranges of silver foxes, beavers, nutria, and other animals. The hotel was a favourite with hikers and artists including Yvonne Auger, who married her third cousin Louis Jammet, owner of a French restaurant in Dublin. The restaurant was a gathering place for artists, writers and actors who were filming at Ardmore Studios in Bray. Actors who could be seen in the restaurant included Orson Wells, Tyrone Power, James Cagney and Peter Ustinov. Louis died in 1964 and Yvonne died on 30 August 1967 on a trip to the United States. Her body was returned to Ireland to be buried alongside her husband in Deansgrange Cemetery. The Mount Maulin fur farm and hotel was sold in 1941 to Kate and Brian Hogan, an engineer who worked on the Drumm Battery Train that operated in the 1930s and '40s from Dublin's Harcourt Street station to Bray. Mount Maulin Hotel was to play a pivotal role when a plane carrying French Girl Guides to a Guide Rally in Dublin crashed on Djouce Mountain in August 1946. The hotel had a French-speaking guest staying at the time of the accident.

FIRE AT GLENCREE REFORMATORY

In May 1935 fire broke out at Glencree Reformatory, and one of the priests of the Oblate Fathers who ran the reformatory rode the 6 miles to Enniskerry police station to raise the alarm. The Dún Loghaire Fire Brigade was dispatched to Glencree. The firemen made the first part of the journey in blinding rainstorms and when they began to climb up the mountains they found the roads covered in a foot of snow. The fire was overcome after two hour's work. Thirty boys sleeping in the burning dormitory were taken to another part of the building to keep them safe.

POWERSCOURT COAT OF ARMS
ON A LARGE RUG

While Lord Powerscourt was commanding troops in North Africa during the Second World War, Lady Powerscourt made herself busy by making a hand-woven rug, 28ft by 18ft. It took eight years of patient work to complete and was valued at hundreds of pounds. It was a copy of one made by the granddaughter of Charles II, except the Powerscourt coat of arms was substituted for the royal coat of arms. The rug was completed in March 1940.

GERMAN BOMBS

On 2 January 1941 a German aircraft ditched two magnetic sea bombs at Glencormac, in the townland of Stilebawn near Enniskerry. The army arrived on-site on 3 January 1941 to diffuse the bombs. Twelve households were evacuated between noon and 2 p.m. and local farmers within a 2- to 3-mile radius were asked to remove livestock. Just before 2 p.m. there were two large explosions as the army detonated the bombs. The explosions were heard in Bray and other towns along the east coast.

COMMANDER OF DESERT RATS AND ENNISKERRY

Major General Gerald Lloyd Verney was born in 1900, at the age of 19 he joined the Grenadier Guards and became aide-de-camp to the Governor of South Australia in 1928. Before the Second World War he was assigned to the Irish Guards, becoming commanding officer of the 2nd Battalion of the Irish Guards Tank Brigade. In 1943 he became general officer commanding the 7th Armour Division in North Africa and reported directly to General Montgomery. He retired in 1948 and purchased Knockmore House near Kilcroney, close to the Dargle River. He wrote a number of books about his time in the army with the Desert Rats of North Africa. He died on 3 April 1957 and is buried at St Patrick's Graveyard, Enniskerry.

GROWING PEAS

In 1954 the general manager of Ever Fresh Foods, Dr Feric, was on holiday in Enniskerry when he met some local farmers in the Mount Maulin area. He persuaded them to grow peas as a commercial venture. The farmers were sceptical at first, but in late May and early June, using a corn drill, the farmers planted a variety of marrow-fat peas called zelka, across 200 acres of land on four farms.

With a dressing of ground limestone and potash, the crop flourished. At harvesting the yield was between 20 and 25 cwt per acre. Five per cent of the crop was sold locally and the remainder was sent to England for freezing and packing.

THE MONSTER
OF LOUGH BRAY

Since the Lough Ness monster was first reputedly spotted in 1933, each tarn or lough in Ireland, England, Scotland and Wales has been said to have a marine creature or monster. On 3 June 1963, a group of hikers in the Wicklow Hills near Glencree observed a strange object floating in Lower Lough Bray. Their leader, with the initials L.R., stated that the creature, with a back like a rhinoceros, emerged from the lake and swam a few yards. Ripples spread out from each side of the creature. He and his fellow hikers observed a head which was like that of a tortoise, only many times bigger, it rose about 3ft above the surface of the water. The overall length of the creature was about 12ft in length. It was dark grey in colour. The sighting lasted for some three minutes, before it disappeared once more.

LADY CHATTERLEY'S LOVER
ENNISKERRY CONNECTION

Mr Justice Laurence Byrne, who was born at Avoca, County Wicklow in 1896, would preside over two major legal cases in England. He was the prosecutor in the case of William Joyce (Lord Haw Haw) in 1945, and the presiding judge in the case Regina v. Penguin Books Ltd in 1960. The prosecution of Penguin Books under the Obscene Publications Act of 1959 was for publishing D.H. Lawerence's, *Lady Chatterley's Lover*. Penguin Books sold 200,000 copies of the book at a face value of 3s 6d. When the case concluded, Justice Byrne retired from the bench and went to live in Enniskerry village. He lived in his native county for four years before moving to Gosfield Hall in Essex where he died on 1 November 1965.

GERMAN WAR CEMETERY

In a disused granite quarry beside Glencree village is the most tranquil cemetery dedicated to German airmen and sailors and a number of civilians who died in Ireland during the First World War and the Second World War. There are 134 graves, looked after by the German War Graves Commission. The cemetery was dedicated on 9 July 1961. The graveyard is dominated by a large granite cross, and fifty-three of the graves are named, while twenty-eight of the graves are of airmen and sailors who could not be identified. Six graves are those of prisoners of war from the First World War. The remainder of the graves are German civilians and prisoners of war who were lost when the SS *Arandora Star* was sunk off Tory Island, County Donegal in 2 July 1940. The ship was assigned the task of transporting German and Italian internees and prisoners of war to Canada, but the ship was sunk, with the loss of 865 lives. The graveyard contains the grave of Dr Hermann Gortz, who committed suicide after the war. It is believed that Dr Gortz was a spy and that he feared he would be handed over to the Soviet Union.

BEQUEST OF COWS AND HENS

On 10 March 1967 Miss Selina (Ina) Adelaide Philippa Boyle of Bushy Park, Enniskerry, died. Miss Boyle was a famous composer and her cousin was Air Chief Marshal Dermot Boyle. Her father, William Boyle, had been rector of Powerscourt parish. Miss Boyle left an estate valued at £64,248, with a stamp duty of £27,826. In her will she left £1,000 and three cows to her herdsman, Mr John Moore. To James Jones of Ballinagee, Enniskerry, her kind friend over many years, she left one cow.

To her maid, Julia Garrett, she left £10 a week for the rest of her life if she was unmarried and in the service of Miss Boyle at the time of her death. Miss Garrett was to be granted the use of the cottage for her life and certain effects therein. Other items, like her collection of musical instruments and sheet music, were granted to museums in England and to the Royal College of Music in London.

AIR-RAID SIREN

During the 1950s, '60s and '70s the Bray Urban Council used the air raid siren installed during the Second World War to call out the Auxiliary Fire Service. The alarm on the siren would send fear and panic into British holidaymakers staying in the town.

HEAVIEST BABY IN IRELAND

The heaviest baby born in Ireland was Michael Anthony Kinch, born to Mary Kinch of Bray on 13 June 1950. Michael weighed 17lb 3oz, or a remarkable 7.7961kgs.

3

FAMOUS FACES

Katie Taylor, the world champion boxer and Cearbheall O'Dáilaigh, the fifth President of Ireland, are associated with the town of Bray. Enniskerry is associated with the member of Parliament the Hon. Henry Grattan, and with Lady Valerie Goulding, one of the founders of the Central Remedial Clinic in 1951, and with Charlie Keegan, world ploughing champion and ancestor of the broadcaster Terry Wogan.

GEORGE ARMSTRONG

George Francis Savage Armstrong was born in Rathfarnham, County Dublin in May 1845, and spent the last few years of his life at Beechhurst, Bray. Armstrong published his first collection of poetry in 1896. This was followed by *Stories of Wicklow*. Armstrong returned to his ancestors' roots in County Down for inspiration for his second novel, *The Ballads of Down*, published in 1901. He died at Beechurst, Bray in 1906, and a selection of his poems was published posthumously in 1919.

REG ARMSTRONG

In November 1979, five-time World Motorcycling Champion Reg Armstrong attended a game shoot near his Ashford home in County Wicklow. On his return home he died in a road accident and was buried at St Patrick's graveyard, Enniskerry.

RICHARD ARCHER

If the mark of an entrepreneur is to move with the times, Richard Archer was such a man. Born near Lough Dan in about 1872, as a young man he became fascinated by motorised transport. In 1904, he established a garage in Dublin with his friend Arthur Hopkins, and three years later he was appointed a Ford agent in Ireland for both cars and tractors. With the shortage of tractors in England during the First World War, Richard seized the opportunity for sales. After the war, he bought the excess stock and sold them second-hand in Ireland. He was a cousin of Richard James Mecredy, who wrote cycling and motoring journals in Ireland. Richard Archer died in 1972.

JANE BARLOW

Barlow was an Irish novelist, the daughter of Revd William Barlow, a provost at Trinity College, Dublin. Her best-known works are *Bogland Studies* (1892), *The End of Elfintown* (1894) and *Irish Idylls* (1892). She died at St Valerie near Bray on 17 April 1917.

CHARLES BARRINGTON

The son of Edward Barrington and Sarah Leadbeater, Charles was born at Fassaroe near Bray in 1834. He was the first Irishman to successfully climb the Eiger Mountain in Switzerland on 11 August 1858. On his farm in Ireland he trained racehorses, including Sir Robert Peel, who went on to glory in the first Irish Grand National in 1870 and won a prize fund of 167 sovereigns. Each year there is a mountain race over Sugarloaf Mountain in County Wicklow for the Barrington trophy, which dates back to the 1870s when Charles Barrington gave a gold watch to the winner. He died on 20 April 1901 and is buried in Mount Jerome Cemetery. Charles' brother, Philip Sydney Barrington, married Elizabeth Shackleton on 30 May 1860. Elizabeth's brother Henry was the father of Sir Ernest Shackleton, the famous Antarctic explorer.

When Ernest Shackleton headed off his voyage to Antarctica, his aunt Elizabeth sent him a bar of soap and a candle.

INA BOYLE

Ina Boyle was born in Enniskerry on 8 March 1889 and she became Ireland's best-known female composer. She got her love of music from her father, the Revd William Boyle the rector of Powerscourt Parish, who made musical instruments.

She studied music in Dublin and showed exceptional talent with both the violin and cello. The two world wars interrupted her musical career, otherwise she could have had an international career. She composed an anthem of death for those killed in the First World War, including her two cousins.

She travelled to London to train under the international composer Ralph Vaughan Williams. Her composition for violin was highly commended at the Olympics of 1948 in London. She was often seen driving her green Morris Minor around the village of Enniskerry. She was the most prolific female composer in Ireland. Her works include 'The Magic Harp' (1919), 'Colin Clout' (1921), 'Gaelic Hymns' (1924), 'Glencree' (1927), 'Wildgeese' (1942) and 'Violin Concerto' (1935). She died of cancer on 10 March 1967, just two days after her seventy-eighth birthday.

REGINALD BRABAZON (12TH EARL OF MEATH)

Reginald Brabazon (1841-1929) was a man with great thoughts and ideas. He was born in 1841 and devoted his life to good works and philanthropy. He gave the Town Hall and the People's Park to the Town of Bray. He was the author of at least ten books and recorded three albums. The Earl of Meath encouraged people to avail of open spaces and take physical exercise, to promote this he proposed an act in Parliament that each local authority should provide open spaces for the enjoyment of the public.

He was appointed High Sheriff of County Dublin and Wicklow. He embraced the Scout movement and became a Chief Scout in Ireland and was on the National Board of Scouting in London.

Lord Meath married Lady Mary Jane Maitland, who was equal to her husband in philanthropy. She was president of the Saturday Hospital Fund, Artesian Dwellings Company which provided cheap housing to the poorer classes of Dublin and Bray. When Lord Meath died in 1929 the public lined the route from Killruddery House to Delgany parish church, including a troop of boy scouts who marched beside the coffin of their Chief. Lord Meath was buried in Delgany graveyard.

HARRY BRADSHAW

Harry Bradshaw was born in Delgany on 9 October 1913. One could say he had golf in is blood. His father, Ned, was a professional golfer at Delgany Golf Club. Harry's brothers, Jimmy, Eddie and Hugh were all professional golfers.

But during the 1940s and '50s, Harry would become a household name in Ireland, winning major titles. He won the Irish PGA Championship ten times between 1941 and 1957. He was the Irish Open Champion winner in 1947 and 1949, and twice he was Dunlop Master Champion, in 1953 and 1955. His best achievement was to come second in the Open Championship of 1949, decided in a playoff.

He played on the Ryder Cup teams of 1953, 1955 and 1957. He held down the position as the Professional Golfer at Kilcroney Golf and Country Club near Bray. He died on 22 December 1990.

JOSEPH CAMPBELL

Joseph Campbell was born in Belfast in 1879. He was a playwright, poet and wrote the lyrics to traditional ballads. He spent some time in London and New York. He lived at Lackandarragh near Enniskerry, where he died on 6 June 1944. He is buried in Deansgrange graveyard, County Dublin. His wife, Nancy Maude, could trace her ancestors back six generations, to the child of King Charles II and his mistress, Nell Gwynne.

SIR HENRY COCHRANE

Sir Henry Cochrane was born in 1836. Thomas Cantrell and Henry Cochrane established a mineral-water bottling company and their brand-name, C&C was born.

Henry became Governor Director of the new mineral aerated water manufacturing company. He held various positions in County Wicklow including High Sheriff and Magistrate, he was a Bray Town Commissioner on the Urban District Council and served a term as chairperson of Bray Town Commissioners. He even found time to be an Alderman in Dublin. He died aged sixty-seven in 1904.

His son, Sir Stanley Cochrane, led an active life, he was a good cricket player and in 1912 he invited the Australian cricket team to tour Ireland and to play at his home, Woodbrook near Bray.

He established Woodbrook Golf Club in 1926 and built a concert hall, where such people as Dame Nellie Melba performed. He became County Wicklow Commissioner of the Boy Scout Association. On the death of his father he became director of the mineral water company C&C.

SEAMUS COSTELLO

Seamus Costello was born in Bray in 1939. He held Republican ideals all his life. He left school at 15 and became a mechanic before going on to become a car salesman in Dublin. At the age of 16 he joined Sinn Féin and during the 1950s, he commanded a unit in the border campaign. In 1957, along with thirteen others, he was arrested in the Glencree area of Enniskerry and committed to Mountjoy Prison for six months. On his released he was interned in the Curragh military camp for two years. While in the camp he master-minded the escape of two high-profile members of the IRA. In 1966 he embarked on a political career and got elected to Bray Urban District Council and Wicklow County Council. He held the positions of Vice President of Official Sinn Féin and staff officer in the Official IRA during the Northern troubles of the 1960s and '70s. He founded the Irish Republican Socialist Party in 1974 and became its chairperson. Seamus Costello was shot while he sat in his car on the North Strand in Dublin on 5 October 1977. At his funeral in Bray the graveside oration was given by Senator Nora Connolly O'Brien, the daughter of James Connolly.

SIR PHILIP CRAMPTON

Sir Philip Crampton was born in 1777. By the time he was twenty-one he was assistant surgeon to the army and appointed surgeon to Meath Hospital. Lord Powerscourt required his services and in return he was offered a patch of ground by the shore of Lough Bray. Mr Crampton got the architect William Morrisson to design a hunting cottage. One of the callers to Lough Bray was the famous Scottish poet and writer, Sir Walter Scott. Sir Philip Crampton wrote a pamphlet on the construction of a bird's eye, for this he became a fellow of the Royal Society of Ireland. He was knighted in 1839 in recognition of his services to the General Forces in Ireland. His Dublin residence was 14 Merrion Square. Prior to his death in 1858, much of his time was spent in the Wicklow Hills.

LUKE CULLEN

Luke Cullen was born near Bray in 1793. He befriended one of the rebels of 1803, Anne Devlin, and the biographer of the United Irishmen, Robert Madden. His first-hand reports of the rebellion of 1798 and the early 1800s were much sought after. He became a monk and is best remembered for his time in Clondalkin where he died in 1859.

WILLIAM DARGAN

William Dargan was born in County Carlow in 1799. He is arguably the greatest railway engineer in Ireland. He designed most of the railway lines laid in the first thirty years of the Irish railway system. He was a member of the Royal Dublin Society and was on the Board of the

National Gallery of Ireland. A statue of Dargan can be found on the lawn of the National Gallery. He was the mastermind behind the Great Industrial Exhibition held in Dublin in 1853. The Exhibition showcased the best of manufacturing and trades in Ireland. Dargan studied railway engineering under Thomas Telford and Isamard Kingdom Brunell. In 1834 he constructed the first railway in Ireland between Dublin and Kingstown (Dún Laoghaire). He found time to live in Bray in a house called Fairy Hill, and later renamed it Galtrim House. While in Bray he was even a Bray Town Commissioner and is given the credit for the development of the Esplanade. His death came in 1867, following a fall from a horse.

DR WENTWORTH ERCK

Descended from Hugenot stock, Wentworth Erck was born in Dublin in 1827. His mother, Elizabeth, was the niece of Sir John Wentworth, the Governor of Nova Scotia. Sir John encouraged the young Wentworth Erck to develop an interest in chemistry and mechanics and a love for astronomy. The Ercks lived at Sherrington, near Shankill, and at Knocklinn on the Ballyman Road near Bray. Young Wentwort Erck built an observatory and was one of the first people in the British Isles to record and make measurements of the moons of Mars. His findings were sent to Mr Arthur Rambaut at the Dunsink Observatory. It is even more remarkable because Mr Erck made his own instruments.

DESMOND FITZGERALD

Desmond Fitzgerald was born in Kerry in 1888 and was a leading member of the Irish Volunteers. He came to the attention of the British forces and they expelled him from Kerry and Dublin, so Desmond moved to Bray in 1915, firstly living at Loreto Villas and then moving to Fairy Hill House on the Killarney Road in 1915. He trained the local volunteers in the People's Park in Bray prior to the Rising in 1916. His wife, Mabel, was secretary to the writer George Bernard Shaw. Desmond arranged a public meeting in Bray to discuss Home Rule and he got a fellow Kerryman, Michael O'Rahilly to speak at it. Desmond was arrested for breaking his restrictions by cycling into County Dublin and he was sent to Mountjoy Prison, but they released him on 31 March 1916, a couple of weeks before the Rebellion. He fought in the GPO, and on his way back home through a number safe houses in Enniskerry and Bray, he was arrested and sentenced to life imprisonment. In 1917 the life sentence was set aside and in 1918, Desmond Fitzgerald was released. On his release he became a Government Minister. His son, Garret, who spent his early years in Bray, would go on to become Taoiseach. The Fitzgeralds sold their house in Bray in 1937. Desmond Fitzgerald died on 9 April 1947.

LADY VALERIE GOULDING

Lady Valerie Goulding was born in 1918. She was one of the foremost campaigners for the disabled in Ireland, fighting for access to all public buildings. In 1951 she was a co-founder of the Central Remedial Clinic, and in the 1960s and '70s she organised Charity Walks to raise funds for the clinic. She married Sir Basil Goulding, a wing commander in the Second World War and a director of the family firm, Gouldings Chemicals, one of the main fertiliser plants in Ireland. Sir Basil and Lady Goulding had a love for the arts. In 1971 they commissioned the architect Scott Tallon Walker to design a cantilevered summer house over the Dargle River, it is considered by some to be one of the finest pieces of architecture in County Wicklow. Lady Goulding died in 2002 and is buried alongside her husband in St Patrick's graveyard, Enniskerry.

YANN RENARD GOULET

Yann Renard Goulet was born in St Nazaire on the Loire in France in 1914. Yann considered himself a true Breton. He studied art and sculpture in Paris. His wartime collaboration with Nazi Germany made him a wanted man and he had to flee France. He arrived in Ireland in 1947 and first settled in Dalkey, before moving to Bray. He took Irish citizenship and began giving art classes, first from his home and later his studio. His fine bronze sculptors can be seen all over Ireland. They are in the grounds of the Customs House in Dublin; the Republican Memorial at Ballyseedy in Kerry, the Christy Ring Memorial in Cork, the crucifix in the church of the Most Holy Redeemer in Bray, and Seamus Costello's headstone in St Peter's graveyard in Little Bray are all his work. Yann was a member of Aosdana. He rode around Bray on his bicycle, and was often seen in the harbour area because of his love of fishing. He was instantly recognisable, with the stub of a cigarette held tightly between his lips and a soft black beret. Yann died in 1999, just two days after his eighty-fifth birthday.

HENRY GRATTAN

In 1782 Parliament granted Henry Grattan a sum of £50,000, with which he bought Tinnehinch House in Enniskerry and a farm at Moyanna located between Vicarstown and Stradbally in County Laois. Tinnehinch House became his principal residence in Ireland. He represented Dublin in the Irish Parliament. After the Act of Union in 1800, he took a seat in the House of Commons in London, representing the constituency of Malton in Yorkshire. He left his Irish home at Enniskerry on 20 May 1820, never to return. His health was failing and he died in London on 4 June 1820 and was buried in Westminster Abbey. His grave is marked with a slab of black marble with the inscription 'Henry Grattan, Died June 4, 1820'. His wish to be buried in Ireland was not carried out, but today he is commemorated in street names, bridges and a number of memorials.

JAMES HAND

Born near Enniskerry, James Hand was an able seaman on HMS *Alert*, which took part in the British Arctic expedition of 1875/76. The expedition was sponsored by the Royal Navy and the Royal Geographical Society. The ships, HMS *Alert* and HMS *Discovery*, left Portsmouth on 29 May 1875 and made their way to the Arctic. At Franklin Bay, under the command of Lieutenant Wyatt Rawson, James Hand and three other men set out on sledges for Polaris Bay. They endured arduous conditions and were soon on reduced rations. They were ill-equipped for the expedition and they all suffered with scurvy. Lieutenant Rawson wrote in his diary, 'Poor Hand had a great desire for lime juice before his death.' James Hand died on 3 June 1876 and Charles Paul died on 29 June 1876. Both men were buried 50 yards north-east of the observatory in Polaris Bay in the Arctic Circle. James Hand is one of two Wicklow men to have their name enshrined in the World Atlas, with James Hand Bay in the Arctic, and Himeville in Africa called after Albert Henry Hime from Kilcoole. A full history of James Hand was written by his great-grandnephew Cyril Dunne, *Buried in the Arctic Ice* (Nonsuch, 2009).

LEWIS WORMSER HARRIS

Lewis Wormser Harris was born in 1812 in Stuggart in Germany. In 1821 Lewis came to Ireland and found employment with Charles Harris, a Dublin watchmaker. Around this time, Lewis adopted the surname Harris. In 1836 he married Caroline Picard and in 1857 he married Juliette Joseph. Lewis and his second wife lived at Royal Marine Terrace, Bray.

Lewis was elected Alderman for Dublin, South Dock Ward, in 1874. He became the first Jew to be elected to public office in Ireland. He was elected Lord Mayor of Dublin and was due to take up his post on 2 August 1876, but he died at his home in Bray on 1 August 1876 aged sixty-four, following a short illness. He is buried in Ballybough and his gravestone is inscribed in Hebrew. His wife, Juliette, died on 12 December 1908.

Eighty years after the death of Lewis Wormser Harris, Robert Briscoe became Dublin's first Jewish Lord Mayor.

JOSEPHINE HEFFERNAN

Josephine Heffernan was born in Dublin in 1876. The family moved to live in Bray and, in 1906, Josephine immigrated to the United States and qualified as a nurse. In 1913 she joined the army and in 1918 was sent to the serve in the First World War. She was chief nurse of the American base hospital at Rimaucourt in France. She lost her ID bracelet. In 2002 it was found by a school boy, who asked his teacher to find Josephine's relatives. What followed was a worldwide search that lasted fifteen years. The search was driven by a researcher and filmmaker with French TV2, the teacher in Rimaucourt and an American historian. The trail came back to Ireland and the town of Bray where Josephine died in 1962. She was buried in St Peters graveyard. On 31 October 2017, Josephine's relatives were reunited with the ID bracelet and the French TV station completed a documentary called 'Josephine H', which aired on 7 January 2018.

PAUL HENRY

Paul Henry is an artists noted for his landscapes depicting the west of Ireland. He was born in Belfast in 1877. He was married twice, first to Grace Henry and then to Mabel Young, both great artists. Paul lived at Carrigoona near Kilmacanogue, and later in Sidmonton Square in Bray. His brother, Robert, was a university lecturer who lived on the Herbert Road, Bray. Paul's work is sought after and in 2006 one of his painting went to auction and sold for €260,000. Paul died in 1958 and is buried in St Patrick's graveyard in Enniskerry. In 2008 the three historical societies of north Wicklow – Bray, Enniskerry and

Kilmacanogue – commemorated the fiftieth anniversary of the passing of Paul Henry.

GEMMA HUSSEY, *NÉE* MORAN

Gemma Hussey was born in Bray in 1938, and her father and mother ran a chemist shop on the Quinsboro Road. James Moran made up cough mixtures on-site and dispensed them in slim six-inch glass bottles. Tablets were dispensed in strong cardboard pill boxes with a wad of cotton wool to protect them. When Gemma was appointed Minister of Social Welfare in 1986 she became the first female government minister from County Wicklow. Subsequently, she was Minister for Labour and Minister of Education. Gemma entered the Senate in 1977 and had been chair of the Women's Political Association from 1973 to 1975, and a member of the Council for the Status of Women.

CHARLIE KEEGAN

The Keegan family have had a farm at Ballinagee near Enniskerry for generations. The name of Charlie Keegan will be etched in the memory of Enniskerry for his victory in the World Ploughing Championships in Austria in 1964. He was the first Irishman to win the event. The biggest crowd ever seen in Enniskerry attended the home-coming of Charlie Keegan in November 1964, a ceremony which included a message from the President of Ireland. Charlie started competitively ploughing following the big snow of 1947. He won local and national ploughing championships, and played a key role in the development of the Powerscourt Ploughing Society. A commemorative plaque and granite bench was unveiled in Enniskerry in 2002, the site is referred to as 'Ploughman's Corner'. Charlie died in 2004, at the age of seventy-seven, and he is buried in St Patrick's graveyard, Enniskerry.

WILLIAM LARMINIE

Born in County Mayo in 1849, William Larminie was an Irish poet and folklorist. He worked in London for the British India Office and retired to Bray in 1887. While living in Bray he published two volumes of poetry – *Glanlua and Other Poems* (1889), and *Fand and Other Poems* (1892) and a collection of folktales called *West Irish Folk-Tales and Romances* (1893). He died in 1900 and is buried in St Patrick's graveyard, Enniskerry.

RICHARD JAMES MCCREADY

Born in 1861 in Ballinasloe, County Galway, Richard McCready came to live in Bray at Vamambrosa. A keen cyclist and track racer, he won major titles in Ireland and England. In 1891 he devised the rules for the only Irish sport at the Olympics, 'Cycle Polo'. He embraced the coming of the motorcar and was one of the first in Ireland to hold a driver's licence. He wrote *The Motoring Atlas of Ireland* and soon this could be found in the glove box of every car in Ireland. He published a weekly magazine on cycling, motorbikes and cars, giving up-to-date information and tips on how to carry out repairs. He was often to be found camping out doors in winter as he suffered from TB. He died while in Dumfries in Scotland in 1927 and is buried in the local graveyard. His son, Ralph, was on the winning Cycle Polo team in the 1908 Olympics. Richard was a good friend of the songwriter and artist, Percy French, and a painting by Percy French hung over the fireplace at Valambrosa. The painting was of nude girls bathing. On one occasion a clergyman arrived at Valambrosa to visit the McCready family. The clergyman was held at the door until another painting could be hung over the fireplace.

DR THOMAS GILLMAN MOORHEAD

Born in Benburb, County Tyrone in 1878, Thomas Moorhead was sent to Aravon in Bray for his early education, and then to Trinity College, where he qualified in 1901 and was elected to the Royal College of Physicians of Ireland in 1905. He worked in the Royal City Hospital Dublin, Sir Patrick Dun's Hospital and a private practice at Prince of Wales Terrace, Bray where his father Dr W.R. Moorhead was the chief medical doctor. During the First World War he joined the Royal Army Medical Corps and served in Cairo. He was elected to the British Medical Association. Mr Moorhead went to England to attend a meeting of the Association in July 1926. While getting off the train at Heuston Station he slipped. When he was helped to his feet, he found that he was blind. He had suffered a bilateral retinal detachment when his head struck the platform. With the assistance of a colleague he continued his clinical duties and gave more time to teaching. He played bridge using Braille-printed cards. He died on 3 August 1960.

CEARBHALL O'DÁLAIGH

Born in Bray in 1911 to Richard Daly, the manager of McCabes Fishmongers at 85 Main Street, Bray, and his wife Una, Cearbhall was educated in Bray National School before the family moved to Vevay Terrace, Bray. Cearbhall studied law and served two terms as Attorney General, before being appointed to the Supreme Court and then to the European Court of Justice. In 1974, following the death of the President of Ireland, Erskine Childers, Cearbhall O'Dálaigh was installed as the fifth President of Ireland. In 1976 he resigned from office after a Government Minister called him 'a thundering disgrace'. Cearbhall retired and lived in Sneem, County Kerry. Where he died in 1978.

FR MICHAEL O'FLANAGAN

Michael O'Flanagan was born in 1876 in County Roscommon. A native Irish speaker, he was brought up with Republican ideals. He joined the priesthood and spent his early years in Roscommon and teaching in Summerhill College in Sligo before being reassigned to Dublin. Fr O'Flanagan recited the opening prayers of the first Dáil and was appointed chaplain to the Oirechetas. In the 1920s Fr O'Flanagan was appointed curate in Bray and during his time there, he undertook the major academic work of editing the Ordnance Survey Notebooks of Ireland. He was also appointed to the Place-names Commission in the 1930s. He died in 1942 and is buried in Glasnevin.

GARRY O'TOOLE

Born in 1968 in Bray, Gary O'Toole went on to represent Ireland in swimming at the two Olympic Games in Seoul and Barcelona. He is a medical doctor and also provides analysis for RTÉ Sport on swimming.

JOSHUA PIM

Another of Bray's sporting stars is Joshua Pim. He was born in Bray in 1869 and went on to become Ireland's best tennis player. He won the Wimbledon Men's Singles title two years in a row, in 1893 and 1894. He also won the Wimbledon Doubles Championships in 1890 and 1893, with his partner Frank Stoker, a brother of Bram Stoker, the author of *Dracula*. Joshua was medical director of Loughlinstown Hospital for forty-two years up to his death on 15 April 1942.

WILLIAM CONYGHAM PLUNKET

William Plunket was born in 1828 and was educated in Dublin and in England. He was appointed chaplain and private secretary to his uncle, the Bishop of Tuam. In 1876 he became the Bishop of Meath and then the Archbishop of Dublin. William Conygham Plunket live at Old Connaught House, Bray and in the summer of 1825 Sir Walter Scott stayed with Lord Plunket. Sir Walter Scott was taken on a carriage drive in the Glencree valley and Sir Walter remarked that the wild and rocky scenery of some parts of the Wicklow Mountains proximate to Dublin, reminded him of some of the scenes of his native Scotland. On retiring as Archbishop, Lord Plunket was appointed a Commissioner of Education, he was instrumental in establishing the Church of Ireland teacher training college and the Kildare Place Society, which set standards of education. There is a memorial to Lord Plunket in Kildare Street, Dublin. He was buried in Mount Jerome, Dublin, upon his death in 1897.

BILLY POWER

Billy Power was a barber and film-maker. In 1918 he founded the Celtic Film Company, which made short films. The actors came from local drama groups and the film scripts were written by Billy Power, probably from stories he heard while cutting hair in his barber shop in Bray. One such film was *Willie Scouts While Jessie Pouts*, a tale of a Fenian who leaves Ireland to join the French Foreign Legion. All the filming was done locally, the sand dunes at Brittas Bay were used for the Foreign Legion locations. While filming *Rosaleen Dhu* at Leopardstown Racecourse, Billy, who was also acting in the production, fell from a horse and died in hospital on 20 June 1920. The last-known print of the film was stored in a house in Little Bray. The house was flooded in 1932 and the film was destroyed.

WILLIAM (LIAM) PRICE

Liam Price was born in Dublin in 1891, and from an early age had his sights set on a legal career. Upon the outbreak of the First World War Liam joined the British Army, only to be appointed to the pay section, based in Cork.

After the war he studied and was called to the bar and appointed a judge. In 1925 he married a medical doctor, Dorothy Stopford, who was one of the foremost doctors in the fight against TB. She also wanted children to be given the BCG injection. Liam Price was appointed a judge in Mullingar, Kilkenny and the Wicklow Circuit. He had a keen interest in folklore and local history. It is said that if an offender came before him in court, he might spend more time discussing the townland where the offender came from than the actual case. Judge Price was an amateur scholar, and between 1945 and 1967 he published seven volumes on the place-names of County Wicklow. This is an invaluable source for local historians. The Bray and Powerscourt townland are included in volume five. Judge Price and his wife lived on Old Connaught Avenue in Bray. Liam became editor of the *Journal of the Royal Society of Antiquaries of Ireland* from 1935 to 1944, and again from 1957 to 1963. Liam Price died in January 1967.

CAPTAIN J.P. 'PADDY' SAUL

Paddy Saul was born in Dublin in 1894, and he would go on to achieve fame as a seaman and aviator. On leaving school, he did not want to go into the family business of coal deliveries, but decided at the age of fifteen to get a Masters Certificate in Marine navigation. During the First World War he joined the Royal Flying Corps and on his return to Ireland he maintained his interest in flying with the Irish Aero Club. His biggest achievement came in 1930 when he was navigator for Charles Kingsford Smith's round-the-world flight in a plane called the 'Southern Cross'. This was to become the first east to west transatlantic flight from Ireland to Newfoundland. The plane took off from the sands at Portmarnock Strand. Afterwards he was asked to take care of the air traffic control system in Ireland. During the Second World War he became and instructor with the Royal Air Force. After the war he retired to live in County Donegal, where he died in 1968. He was buried in St Patrick's graveyard in Enniskerry. Thirty years after his death, An Post issued a stamp to commemorate a great aviator.

HOLDEN STODART

Holden Stodart was born in 1883 and lived in Blackrock, County Dublin. He was an employee of the Guinness brewery, but on his days off and weekends worked for the St John's Ambulance Service. During the Easter Rising he was stationed at Baggot Street Hospital. He got a call to attend a wounded soldier at Northumberland Road, when the stretcher party arrived they were caught in the crossfire between the soldiers and the rebels. Holden Stodart was killed, and as a mark of remembrance the staff at Guinness and the St John's Ambulance Service made a collection and raised £732. This money was given to the Duke of Connaught Auxiliary Hospital for wounded soldiers in Bray and they named a ward after Holden Stodart. The adjoining ward was called the Guinness Ward. Holden Stodart is buried in Mount Jerome graveyard in Dublin.

KATIE TAYLOR

Katie Taylor was born in Bray in 1986 and was educated at St Killian's in the town. Her love for boxing has seen her take World, European and National titles. In 2012 she went on to win an Olympic gold medal in the 60kg class. She was the flag bearer for Ireland at the opening ceremony of the 2012 Olympics in London. Katie has won Sportsperson of the Year awards and Bray Civic awards. Her home-coming from the Olympics attracted over 80,000 people to Bray seafront, where she was accompanied by her father and trainer, Peter. Peter can be seen at the ringside at all her contests. Katie was instrumental in getting a new training facility for Bray Boxing Club following her Olympic title. She has appeared on the panel of RTÉ Sport programmes for World, European and National boxing competitions. Prior to taking up boxing, Katie put on the green jersey to play soccer for Ireland and was a good Gaelic footballer in her local club. Katie now has her sights set on the Olympic Games in 2016.

FR AIDAN TROY

Aidan Troy was born in Bray in 1945 and educated locally. At the age of 19 he joined the Passionist Order and spent time in Rome, before returning to Ireland to take charge of the Holy Cross parish in Belfast. In 2001 and 2002 Fr Troy came to public attention when, with the help of the RUC and local parents, he escorted primary school children from their homes to the Holy Cross School in Ardoyne in Belfast, through vicious and violent loyalist protest, for a period of four months. Today, Fr Troy is the head of St Joseph's church in the heart of Paris.

BOLTON CHARLES WALLER

Bolton Waller was born in Cobh in County Cork. The family moved to Bray, first settling on the Meath Road and then at Carlton Terrace. In 1926, Bolton Charles Wallace, now studying at Trinity College Dublin, wrote an essay called 'Paths to Peace'. This document was a submission to a competition following the First World War, when nations were looking for a better way to deal with international conflict. An American businessman had created a prize fund of £3,000, with a first prize of £1,000 and the balance shared out among the top ten essays. Bolton won the £1,000 and his document, 'Paths to Peace' was adopted by the League of Nations, and subsequently by the UN. Bolton took holy orders and, after a time in Rathmines, became rector of St John's church in Clondalkin. He died in 1936 and is buried in the local graveyard in Clondalkin.

ISAAC WELD

Isaac Weld was born in Dublin in 1774. He was an author and travel writer, his best work, *A Vacation Tour in the United States and Canada* was first published in 1855. He drew pen sketches of the places he visited. In 1802 he married Alexandra Hope and had a daughter called Esther. He wrote an historical sketch of the scenery of Killarney in 1815 and he followed this with a historical account of his home, Ravenswell, near Bray, in 1817. He died at Ravenswell on 8 August 1956 and is buried in Mount Jerome.

SOPHIA ST JOHN WHITTY

A teacher, designer, artist, and woodcarver, Sophia St John Whitty was born in 1877 in Dublin, but she lived at Oldbawn in Old Connaught, near Bray. She was one of the first women to be appointed a teacher under the new Agriculture and Technical Instruction (Ireland) Act 1899, which established vocational schools in Ireland. She died in 1924, just before the new Vocational Act was passed in 1930. Bray Vocational Educational Committee was the first VEC established under the 1930 Act. Miss Whitty and her friend, Kathleen Scott, are best remembered for their work with the Bray Art Furniture Industry, or the Bray Woodcarvers. The woodcarvers gave technical instruction in fretwork to the wounded soldiers in the Princess Patricia Hospital and the Duke of Connaught Hospital two days a week during the

First World War. The First World War saw the demise of the Bray Woodcarvers, with many of the carvers going off to war. The carvers saw orders dwindle, even though Miss Scott and Miss Whitty tried to keep it going. The final chapter came with the death of Miss Whitty in 1924. The best display of the woodcarver's work can be seen in Christ Church on Church Road, Bray.

SISTER MARY CLARE, NÉE EMMA CLARE WITTY

Emma Witty was born in Enniskerry in 1912. She joined the Community of St Peter at Woking, Surrey, and was professed in 1915 in the order of the Society of the Holy Cross. She first went to Korea in 1923, returning to England when the Second World War forced the withdrawal of missionary staff. She returned to Korea in January 1947, and died in an internment camp in North Korea on 6 November 1950.

MARY JOSEPHINE WOGAN

Mary Wogan, an aunt of the late BBC broadcaster Terry Wogan, was born at Church Hill, Enniskerry in 1894. She became a nurse in the Red Cross Hospital in Dublin Castle during the First World War and the Easter Rising. She treated James Connolly in the days before he was executed. After the war she took up a nursing post in England, and she was there when the Second World War broke out. Miss Wogan returned to Ireland in 1959 and worked as a nurse in St Brigid's, a TB hospital at Kilternan, and she also worked at a hospital in Dublin. She died at a nursing home in Bray in 1980 at the age of eighty-six and is buried at Curtlestown near Enniskerry.

4

MANSIONS, HOUSES AND HOTELS

CHARLEVILLE

Charleville lies in the shadow of Powerscourt House on R755, south of Enniskerry. The estate came into the hands of the Monck family through the marriage of Charles Monck, a Dublin barrister and MP for Innnistogue, County Kilkenny, to Agenta Hitchcock in 1705. Thomas the second son of this marriage, was father of Charles Stanley Monck, made 1st Baron Monck in 1797 and 1st Viscount Monck in 1801. The latter title came as a reward for securing his vote in the Act of Union. The original Charleville House was burnt to the ground in 1792 and Whitmore Davis was called upon to design a new house, which was built in the 1790s. It was then remodel in the 1820s by the 2nd Viscount, who was became Earl of Rathdowne in 1822.

The earldom of Rathdowne died with the first earl, who had nine daughters but no son. The 4th daughter, Elizabetha Louisa, married her cousin, the fourth Viscount Monck. He had a distinguished political career and was appointed the first Governor General of British America, at the time the Dominion of Canada, in 1867. William Gladstone visited the house in 1887 and he planted a tree near the house. Edith, Viscountess Monck, the widow of the fifth Viscount, was the last of the family to live at Charleville, which was closed up after her death in 1929.

It was put up for sale in the 1930s and bought by Mr Donald Brooke Davies and his wife, Mary, in 1941. They ran a highly successful clothing business from one of the stable buildings at Charleville. They refurbished the house and returned the gardens to their former glory. In 1978, they decided to leave Ireland for a home in England and they sold Charleville to Mr and Mrs Hugh Hawthorn. In the 1990s the house was sold to the property developer Mr Ken Rohan and his wife Belinda.

POWERSCOURT HOUSE

By far the most important house in the district, it was originally built on the lands of Eustace Le Poer, whose name was corrupted to give us Powerscourt.

Queen Elizabeth I granted Sir Richard Wingfield the land of Fercullen and the parish of Stagonil. In 1730 Richard Cassels was asked to remodel the sixty-eight-room Powerscout Castle. Cassels was a busy builder at that time and the work on the new villa of Powerscourt was not completed until 1741. Set in stunning landscape with a back drop of Sugarloaf Mountain, the house was ready for its first royal visit, and King George IV came in August 1821. Lord Powerscourt had his head gamekeeper shoot a buck deer and it was presented to the royal party on their arrival at Kingstown.

Lord Powerscourt had a dam created at the head of the waterfall. On the instruction of Lord Powerscout a sluice gate was to be opened, to show the waterfall in full flow. The King was to stand on the bridge constructed below the fall. The King was delayed, meeting guests in Powerscourt House, and he never made it to the bridge to see the waterfall in full flow. On the day Powerscourt estate workers opened the sluice gate the flow of water washed away the wooden bridge.

In 1897, the Duke of York considered buying Powerscourt as his Irish palace but Lord Powerscourt was reluctant to sell. In the 1930s Lord Powerscourt tried to sell Powerscourt to the Irish Free State (Saorstát Éireann), but his offer was refused.

In 1961, Powerscourt Estate was sold to the Slazenger family. The house was destroyed by fire in November 1974, and in just over twenty years the house was re-roofed and was opened to the public by President Mary Robinson in 1997. The house has been the location for many films such as *Henry V* (1944), *The Count of Monte Cristo*, *King Arthur*, *Barry Lyndon*, and many more. Today, Powerscourt House is the number one visitor attraction in County Wicklow. Part of the house is devoted to retailers selling clothing and furniture. It is also the home of Tara's Palace, a beautiful handcrafted wooden doll's house. On payment of a fee the landscaped grounds can be visited. There is also a garden centre, hotel and golf course within the Powerscourt Estate.

BUSHY PARK

Bushy Park, Enniskerry has changed hands a number of times since the early 1800s. Initially, it was the family home of Colonel Hugh Howard and his son Ralph. The mansion was built 1815 for the colonel, brother of the Earl of Wicklow. Hugh was a Member of Parliament who voted for the Act of Union and was granted the position of Post Master General of Ireland.

During the King's visit to Powerscourt in 1821 Lord Powerscourt invited many of his neighbours, including Colonel Hugh Howard of Bushy Park, to attend the King. The King, looking out one of the windows at Powerscourt, saw the house at Bushy Park and, turning to Lord Powerscourt said, 'Whose house is that opposite? It ought not to be there'. Meaning that it did not add to the beauty of the landscape. Colonel Howard joined the conversation at this point. 'Oh, but your Majesty, that is my house'. The King said, 'I don't care whose house it is, it ought not to be there'.

On the death of Colonel Hugh Howard the house passed to his son, Sir Ralph Howard. Ralph's sister, Theodosia, married the fifth Lord Powerscourt, while his other sister, Frances, married William Hayes Parnell. Sir Ralph died in 1873 and the property passed to his brother-in-law, Parnell. It was William Parnell who laid out the Earl's and Lady's Drives on Powerscout Estate. William and Frances Howard had two children, Catherine and John Henry Parnell, the father of Charles Stewart Parnell. On the death of William Parnell, the house passed to Sir Philip Crampton and his son, John, who was a British diplomat who served in Washington, St Petersburg, Brussels and Vienna. John married Victoria Balfe, the daughter of the Irish author and music composer, Michael William Balfe. After the Cramptons, the house was occupied by Judge William N. Keogh, who presided over the trials of the Fenians Thomas Luby, John O'Leary, Charles Kickham, and O'Donnovan Rossa.

Another musical family lived at Bushy Park, Revd Boyle, rector of Powerscourt Parish, and his daughter Ina, a famous composer who represented Ireland in music at the London Olympics in 1948. Revd Boyle married Phillipha Jephson, and a number of Jephson family members lived at Bushy Park. They are buried in St Patrick's graveyard in Enniskerry.

Edward Nicholas Bisgood, a London businessman, purchased Bushy Park, he was followed by his son, Richard Bertram, whose headstone in St Patrick's graveyard describes him as a sportsman, soldier and dedicated countryman. His wife, Audrey is described on the same headstone as a creative, artistic and accomplished plants woman. In 1997, the singer Chris De Burgh and his wife, Diane, became the owners of Bushy Park.

KILRUDDERY HOUSE

Kilruddery House was built on the lands belonging to St Mary's Abbey of Dublin on the road between Bray and Greystones. For over 400 years it was the family home of the Earls of Meath, the Brabazon family. Guests entertained at Kilruddery include Prime Minister William Gladstone and Robert Baden Powell, founder of the Scouting movement.

The Earl of Meath established the Industrial Schools in Bray and Blackrock, County Dublin. In the early 1900s artisans' dwellings were built in Little Bray, and the streets were named after members of the Brabazon family. For example, Maitland Street is named after the Countess of the 12th Earl of Meath, Lady Mary Jane Maitland. For many generations the best medical care in Dublin and Wicklow was provided in Meath Hospital in Dublin, while the elderly got the best of care in Brabazon Home in Sandymount. Even the healthy could contribute to the Hospital Sunday Fund. Its first president was Lord Brabazon himself. Many of the open spaces in London, Dublin and Bray owe a debt to Lord Meath, who encouraged town councils to provide parks for the enjoyment of the public. The People's Park Bray was presented by Lord and Lady Brabazon as a gift to the Bray Town Commissioners in 1881. They also donated the iconic Town Hall.

GLENCORMAC

Many different versions of the name Glencormac have appeared over the years, including Glencormick and Glencormack. In recent times a legal case was thrown out of court over the spelling of Glencormac. It is located on the Bray side of Kilmananogue, where the Avoca Handweavers outlet and garden centre stands. The original house was built for James Jameson, the son of John Jameson and Margaret Haig. John was the founder of the famous whiskey distillery that carries his name, while Margaret Haig came from another Scottish whiskey family. James was born in 1806 and he married a woman called Lucy Cairns. They built a fabulous house and landscaped the grounds. Today there is still a marvellous Montorey Cypress tree on the grounds, planted in 1874. James' brother, Andrew, was the grandfather of Guglielmo Marconi, founder of the Wireless Telegraph & Signal Company which carries his name. On the death of James in 1899 and his wife Lucy in 1907, the property passed to Francis Bellingham Jameson. He was given the middle name Bellingham because he was born at Castle Bellingham, County Louth. Francis married Margaret Cardew.

Francis died in Pau in the south of France, and on the death of Margaret, Glencormac was put up for sale in December 1954, where it was bought by the Longford businessman, John Doris, who opened it as a hotel. In June 1965, Sir Albert Margai, the Prime Minister of Sierra Leone, dined at the hotel. In the mid-1960s the hotel was destroyed by fire. In the 1980s the ruin was bought by Donal Pratt, who had established Avoca Handweavers Ltd in 1984. He developed an outlet for selling handwoven garments, handmade confectionary, plants and a successful café. Today it is one of the most successful businesses in north Wicklow, with another outlet in Powerscourt House.

KILCRONEY HOUSE

Kilcroney House was built for Humphrey Lloyd, a provost of Trinity College, on his death it was sold to Matthew Peter D'Arcy, the owner of the Anchor Brewery in Dublin and Member of Parliament for County Wexford. He was married twice. He had three sons from his first marriage, John, William and James who was a captain in the Rifle Brigade and was killed in 1918. He had five daughters and one son with his second wife, his son, Matthew Stephen, was killed at the Siege of Mafeking in the Anglo-Boer War.

Kilcroney then became the home of Alfred West and his wife, Florence Levey, and their four children, Cyril, Hazel, Harold and Aubrey. Alfred was born in 1851 and was a lieutenant in the Wicklow Militia, and High Sheriff of County Wicklow, who died in 1919. His wife, Florence, was a keen gardener, and in 1928 she displayed her Irish Daffodils at the Royal Horticultural Hall in Westminster, in London. She won a total of seventeen prizes; nine first place prizes, five seconds and three third places. She also won the Barr Memorial Daffodil Cup for the best daffodils in the show and was awarded the Horticultural Society medal for winning the most prizes. Today, the driveway to Kilcroney House is lined with daffodils.

CORKE ABBEY

The abbey is in the townland of Great Corke, just north of the River Dargle and Bray Commons. In 1460 the property was held by Walter Harold of Old Connaught, and it had been granted to him by Reginald Talbot, a descendent of the Earl of Ormonde. Over the following centuries the property was to change hands a number of times, being held by the Walshes of Ballyman, Peter Talbot, the Walshes of

Shanganagh, and by the eighteenth century a Mr Arthur Bushe resided at Corke and his descendents sold it to Theophilus Jones, a gentleman farmer. In 1799 he wrote a paper for the Royal Dublin Society on the 'use of clover and potatoes for swine'; he had fed a group of hogs clover and potatoes and they had gained more weight than another group of hogs on a different diet. The meat from the hogs fed with clover and potatoes was far superior.

In 1811 Edward Wingfield, the son of Lord Powerscourt, acquired Corke Abbey, and in 1819 Edward Wingfield's daughter, Harriet, married Sir William Verner, who held the property until it was sold to Mr David Frame, who had just sold Bray Head House. David Frame started the first lamp factory in Ireland, Solus Teo, in 1935, at Corke Abbey. In 1982 Nypro Ltd took over part of the Solus Factory, and in 1984 the Garveys of Drogheda bought the lamp division of Solus and the new company was called Solus Lamps Ltd.

Within the grounds of Corke Abbey Martello Tower Number 3 was built in 1804. The tower was demolished in 1911. Tower Number 1 was on Bray Seafront, but this tower was demolished in 1863. Tower 2, overlooking Bray Harbour, the former home of U2 frontman, Bono, is still standing.

RAVENSWELL

Ravenswell lies north of the River Dargle and Bray Commons. The name 'Ravenswell' or 'Raven's Well' first appears on Duncan's Map of 1821, but in written documents it dates back to 1684 as 'Regans Well'. In the late 1700s and early 1800s it was the home of Clothworthy Rowley, the Member of Parliament for Downpatrick. In 1813 it was purchased by the explorer and travel-writer Issac Weld, who lived there until 1856. He was one of the secretaries and Vice President of the

Royal Dublin Society. On Weld's death the house was purchased by Richard Dease, who rented the property to Jonathan Whitby Christian and his wife, Mary Thomas. Their eight children must have enjoyed the house and the adjoining 46 acres of farmland. Jonathan was called after his uncle Jonathan who was the Inspector General of the Irish Coastguard. His cousin, Charlotte Mabel Christian, married Charles Putland of San Souci, Bray, now Loreto Convent. Jonathan split his time between Ravenswell and his house in Merrion Square Dublin. He was called to the bar in 1834 and held a number of legal posts including Solicitor General for Ireland, Justice of the Common Pleas, Lord Justice of the Court of Appeal, and Queen's Counsel. Jonathan died in 1887 but had left Ravenswell many years earlier.

Ravenswell was put up for sale in 1882 by Anna Maria O'Reilly-Dease, the widow of Richard Dease, the eminent Dublin physician. Richard died about 1821 and prior to the sale in 1882 Anna Marie lived in Ravenswell with her two daughters, Anna and Mathilda, and her son, Matthew O'Reilly-Dease, who was born in 1819. Matthew became a barrister and Member of Parliament for County Louth. In 1843 he was elected a life member of the Royal Dublin Society and he kept his award-winning Kerry cattle herd at Bray. He owned, in total, 2,366 acres in counties Louth, Cavan, Meath, Mayo, Dublin and Wicklow. In 1857 he engaged the architect Sandham Symes to construct two greenhouses at Ravenswell, and in 1859 he won a gold medal for cereals grown in Bray. In 1861 he called for the Botanic Gardens in Dublin to be open on a Sundays so that it could be enjoyed by the public. Matthew died in 1887, but he had sold Ravenswell to Lord Brabazon four years earlier. Prior to the sale Matthew had employed a caretaker, Mrs Sweeney, to look after the house and when Lord Brabazon bought the house he continued to employ Mrs Sweeney. In 1879 Mrs Sweeney was murdered and her body was thrown down the well behind the house. A person named Michael Tiernan was charged with her murder.

Lord Brabazon was the eldest son of the Earl of Meath and he lived at Ravenswell up to 1898, when the contents of the house were auctioned off. Included in the auction were 150 bottles of champagne, 150 bottles of choice claret, and 150 bottles of fine wine, including burgundy, sherry and foreign liquors. The house was bought by the Sisters of Charity, who opened the Holy Family Convent. The architect, Henry William Byrne, designed a new girl's national school that cost £2,343, in 1900. The buildings were used during the summer months as a holiday home for working girls of Dublin run by the Sisters of Charity. A flag day was held in Dublin each year at the time of the Spring Show in the RDS, and the funds raised help to fund the holiday home for that year.

OLDCOURT

Oldcourt lies off the Bray/Greystones Road but is hidden in the valley of Swanbrook River. The site was designed as a pleasure garden for the Brabazon family and it contains a Norman castle and a lake. Six generations of the Edwards family have lived at Oldcourt. Most of this family is buried in St Paul's graveyard near Bray Bridge. The family contained farmers, soldiers and even a poet. John Edwards, born in 1751, was compared to Tom Moore, who wrote the great ballads of Ireland such as 'The Meeting of the Waters' about the Wicklow Rivers the Avonmore and Avonbeg. John Edwards also used a Wicklow theme for his work, 'Kathleen of Glendalough', which depicts a girl trying to woo St Kevin. In 1820 he wrote an essay on ways to improve banknotes, from paper quality to preventing forgery. Mr Edwards held a rank in the Wicklow Militia in 1798 and was also in the Light Dragoon Guards, with the rank of lieutenant-colonel. The ancestors of the Edwards family include the King of Wales, Rhodri Mawr. Other people to live at Oldcourt include Mr Ferrier of the Dublin merchants, Ferrier Pollack, and Harry Holfeld, best known for his company H.R. Holfeld on the Stillorgan Road, a distributor of water pumps in Ireland.

TINNAHINCH

The house was built in 1770 by Lord Powerscourt as a coaching inn. Arthur Young, the English agricultural writer, stayed at the inn on his tour of Ireland in 1777. In 1780 he published a detailed account of life in Ireland. The book was reprinted in 1897 and in 1925. In 1782 Henry Grattan was offered the Viceregal Lodge in Dublin but refused the offer, instead he accepted an offer of £50,000 which he used to purchase two estates; Tinnahinch near Enniskerry, and Moyanna, County Laois. He also built a shooting lodge near Dunrally in County Laois. Henry Grattan stated that he could make the journey from Tinnehinch to the Parliament building in Dame Street in Dublin in a half an hour. At the time of the Act of Union Henry Grattan stood down from political life, but his friends encouraged him to take a seat in the House of Commons. It was on a journey to the House of Commons in 1820 that he died. His friends ignored his request to be buried in Ireland and instead he was buried in Westminster Abbey. The Irish poet, Thomas Moore, was a good friend of Grattan. While visiting Tinnahinch he wrote the ballad 'The Last Rose of Summer'. A visitor to the house once remarked how a big beech tree was dangerously near the house. Henry Grattan replied 'I have often thought that I must have the house moved'.

Tinnahinch remained a Grattan home up to 1943, when the contents of the house were sold at public auction. Mr Harris removed the roof of original house and built a new house in the grounds. The house was subsequently sold to Mr Duff, Mr Poole and Mr Murphy, who all carried out extensive landscaping and invested a lot in maintaining the house. The house and grounds cover about 50 acres, with a half mile of fishing rights for trout along the Dargle River.

OLD CONNAUGHT HOUSE
AND OLD CONNA HILL

The area between Shankill, Rathmichael and Ballyman was owned, prior to the 1780s, by the Roberts and Walsh families. About 1780, Old Connaught House was built for William Conyngham Plunket, a barrister, King's Counsel, Member of Parliament, Privy Counsellor, Justice of Common Pleas, and Lord Chancellor. He was succeeded by his son, Thomas. Thomas' daughter, Katherine, was born in 1820 and died in 1932 and, according to the *Guinness Book of Records*, is the oldest woman to live in Ireland, dying aged 111 years. When Thomas died in October 1866 his brother John Span Plunket, a barrister and Crown Prosecutor of the Munster Circuit, inherited Old Connaught House.

John's son, the Revd William Conyngham Plunket (4th Baron), also lived at Old Connaught. Between 1876 and 1884 he was Bishop of Meath and in 1884 became Archbishop of Dublin. In 1863 he married Anne Lee Guinness, the daughter of Sir Benjamin Guinness, and got a dowry of £49,000. The money was used to carry out improvements to the property at Old Connaught including building a walled garden that is now Festina Lente. The couple had six children, William (5th Baron), Elizabeth, Benjamin, Olive, Kathleen and Ethel. A monument to William, the 4th Baron, stands beside the Department of Agriculture in Kildare Street. William died in 1897 and the property fell to his son, also called William, who was in the diplomatic service and was attaché at the British Embassy in Rome. He was also private secretary to the Lord Lieutenant of Ireland between 1900 and 1904, and later served as private secretary to the Governor of New Zealand. In New Zealand, Lord Plunket's wife, Lady Victoria, established in 1907 the 'Plunket Society', a society that provides health services to mothers and their babies. William's son, Terrence was Royal Air Force pilot, but on a private visit to California in 1938 he died in an air crash. Old Connaught and its adjoining property, Wallcot, were purchased in 1956 by the Irish Christian Brothers.

Old Connaught House was the monks' residence and St Brendan's Secondary School was housed in the former Wallcot House. Sir Richard Morrision, an architect who had designed many of the houses in the area, lived at Wallcot. In 2000, Old Connaught House was sold and the eighteenth-century listed building was converted into twenty-five apartments.

Near Old Connaught House is Old Conna Hill, and for more than a century this was the home of the Riall family. The Riall family originally came from Wales and they settled in Clonmel in County Tipperary, where they had their own private bank. Charles, the second son of Sir Phineas Riall, the great explorer and Governor of Grenada, lived at Annerville, County Tipperary. In 1837, Charles married Anne Roberts, the daughter of the previous owner of the Old Connaught property. Charles's son Phineas (1803-1884) invested thousands of pounds into the grounds and walled garden, and he won many medals and cups from the Royal Dublin Society and Horticultural Societies for crops, trees and plants grown at Old Conna Hill. When Phineas died in 1884 the farm was run by Captain Lewis Riall. Lewis died in 1930 and left an estate of £6,221, and Old Conna Hill passed to two of his three daughters. First was his eldest daughter, Olive, who died a spinster, and then to the younger sister, Violet Maud.

After Violet's death the property passed to a cousin, Claude Phineas Bookey Riall, who also owned Ballyorney House near Enniskerry. Claude died at Old Conna Hill in 1953 and the contents of the house were sold at auction. The items included Turkish rugs, paintings by Dutch and Italian Masters, and Irish landscape paintings. The house was purchased by an Englishman, Mr Parkes, who opened a luxury hotel, within a few years the hotel was run by Mr Stewart Roberston from Florida. In 1961, Mr Roberston sold the hotel to another American consortium who appointed Count Cyril McCormack the son of the Irish Singer Count John McCormack, as the hotel's general manager. The rooms in the hotel were called after literary and cultural figures such as Dean Swift, James Joyce, Tom Moore, Oscar Wilde and George B. Shaw.

In 1961 Mr Kenneth Besson, a director of the Old Conna Hill Hotel, was asked by Córas Iompair Éireann to take charge of its Hotel Division. The American actress, Kim Novak, stayed at Old Conna Hill in 1963, while filming *Of Human Bondage* at Ardmore Studio. Kim had a fear of flying, so she took the boat from New York to England, she then drove her white Jaguar to Liverpool to catch the ferry to Ireland. The white Jaguar became a major talking point around Bray and Enniskerry. In 1984, the hotel closed and it was acquired by Aravon Private School, which had been established in Bray in 1862.

PALERMO HOUSE

Palermo House on Old Connaught Avenue, near Bray, was one of the Synge Hutchinson family homes prior to the Act of Union. The Hutchinson family can trace their lineage back to Samuel Hutchinson, an ensign in the regiment of Lord Forbes at the Battle of the Boyne. Francis Hutchinson was created a baronet of Ireland in 1872 and acquired the property at Palermo. His son, James, had no children, and the property at Palermo was acquired by Sir Francis' nephew, the Revd Sir Samuel Synge Hutchinson, who was married twice. His eldest son, Francis, married, Louisa, the daughter of Hon. Francis Hely Hutchinson, and they had two sons and a daughter. Francis' sister, Sophia, married a Royal Naval captain, Coote Hely Hutchinson, brother of the Earl of Donoughmore, and they lived at Plamero.

When the Synge Hutchinson family left Palermo house it was sold to Mr Fitzpatrick who ran the Wicklow Hills Bus Company in Enniskerry. The House was used between 1941 and 1977 as a glove factory by Ermo Ltd, making high-quality ladies gloves. The company had a display in the Intercontinental Hotel in Ballsbridge and a pair of gloves was bought by Princess Grace of Monaco during her visit to Ireland in 1965. The house lay idle for a number of years before it was demolished to make way for a housing estate.

WOODBROOK

The title Baron of Woodbrook was created in 1760 and granted to George Ribton, who was Lord Mayor of Dublin between 1747 and 1748. On the death of George the title passed to his son, George, and then to John Sheppy Ribton, who was an army man and fought alongside Arthur Wellesley, the 1st Duke of Wellington. John was wounded four times in his nine-year military career and he retired on half pay in 1818. John turned his hand to farming and became first master of the Bray Hunt. His first wife, Emily, died in 1832, when her carriage overturned at Woodbrook. John died in 1877 and his son, George, lived at the Gray Fort in Kilcoole, so Woodbrook was put up for sale, where it was bought by Henry Cochrane, a director of

Cantrell & Cochrane, the mineral water manufacturing company in 1921. Woodbrook Golf Club was founded and was affiliated to the Golfing Union of Ireland in 1926. The club has hosted the Barton Cup and the Irish Open Championships.

COTTAGES AND HOMES OF THE DARGLE VALLEY

Hidden behind boulders, walls and small groves of trees, we find numerous cottages in the Dargle Valley. Many hold secrets of the past. One such cottage is Bahana Cottage, appreciated for its solitude by the author James J. Gaskin, aka J.J. Gaskin or Professor Gaskin, in 1846, when he wrote his book *Geography and Sacred History of Syria and Palestine*. He also wrote *The Letters and Speeches of the Lord Lieutenant Lord Carlisle*, *Geography made Easy* (1842), and *Irish Varieties: A History of Dublin and North Wicklow*. This was first published in 1869 and reprinted in 1874 and 1887.

In 1749, Henry Booth rented lands at Bahana from Lord Powerscourt with an annual rent of £35. He also had to provide Lord Powerscourt with two fat geese and six horses.

VALCULSA

Another house along the Dargle Valley is Valclusa, the former home of Judge Edward Falconer Litton, who was born in Dublin on 18 December 1828. He was called to the bar in 1847 and took silk in 1874. He was then elected, in 1880, as a Liberal Member of Parliament for County Tyrone. In 1881 he was appointed a member of the new Land Commission. On the retirement of Mr Justice O'Hagen Mr Litton was appointed a judge in the Supreme Court. On 27 November 1890, Justice Litton died at Valclusa. The Briscoe family, well-known all over Ireland for breeding cattle and dogs, bought Valculsa. Isabella Briscoe won many prizes with her terrier 'Bashful Brenda of Valculsa'. In the 1950s a Mr Frank Gray lived at Valclusa and he won a prize fund of £4,100 in a 'Radio Review' crossword, the highest sum paid in any Irish crossword puzzle. The prize was presented by the Lord Mayor of Dublin at the Theatre Royal in 1958. Valclusa was sold in 1964 and was bought by Paul D. MacWeeney, the sports editor for *The Irish Times*. Paul's grandfather was an editor with the *Freeman's Journal*. Paul was born in Dublin in 1909 and would excel in many sports. His first job in 1929 was as a reporter for the *Irish Independent*.

In 1931 he was offered a job with *The Irish Times*, reporting on rugby, golf, boxing, hockey and squash. He was responsible for the formation of the Irish Table Tennis Association in the 1920s, and at the age of 14 he held the Irish Table Tennis Championship, and would do so for six years. He played hockey for Monkstown and Three Rock Rovers. He was not a bad golfer either and played with a single-figure handicap. He took up squash and was Irish Champion in 1941-1942. Paul died in 1983. Valclusa was put up for sale in 1998 with a price tag of £750,000. The house was designed by the architect Richard Morrison, who wanted it to be called Valcluse, but Judge Litton thought that Valclusa sounded better.

SUMMERHILL HOUSE

Summerhill, Enniskerry, now a hotel and spa, will always be associated with the name William Richard Le Fanu, who was the younger brother of Joseph Thomas Sheridian Le Fanu, the Victorian ghostwriter. William, Thomas and their sister Catherine were born at the Royal Hibernian Military School at Chapelizod in Dublin, where their father Revd Thomas was the chaplain. The family moved to Abington, near Limerick City where the Revd Thomas became rector. For generations afterwards the Le Fanu called their houses 'Abington'. William got a reputation as an engineer for building viaducts, and he was consulted about most of the railway viaducts built in Ireland, all of which he would recalled in his book *Seventy Years of Irish Life: The Life of a Railway Engineer*. After becoming the chief engineer with the Cork and Bandon Railway Company, he took a post with the Dublin, Wicklow and Wexford Railway Company. In 1857 he married Henrietta Barrington, the daughter of Sir Matthew Barrington of Limerick. William and Henrietta had ten children, eight boys and two girls.

The eldest son, Thomas, became private secretary to the Chief Secretary of Ireland, he was also Commissioner of the Office of Public Works (OPW) between 1913 and 1926, and he was responsible for the rebuilding of public buildings following the Easter Rising and the Civil War. From 1933 to 1936 he was president of the Royal Society of Antiquaries of Ireland. In 1924 he wrote a book, *Memoir of the Le Fanu Family* that traces the Le Fanu history from Huguenots who arrived in Dublin in the 1730s. He lived at Abington on the Killarney Road, Bray. Thomas died in 1945.

VIOLET HILL

Violet Hill House on the Herbert Road was built in 1836 for Mr Hartshorn as a private boarding school. The school had one selling point for parents: no summer vacations. For a short period prior to 1863 Judge William N. Keogh lived at Violet Hill. In 1863 it was sold to Mr Edward Lysaght Griffin, the son of the Bishop of Limerick. Edward was a leading barrister and registrar of the Friendly Societies of Ireland. He refurbished the twelve-bedroom house and walled garden in 1863 at a cost of £5,000. He later added stables at a cost of £1,200. In 1863 he married Beatrice Cruddock and they had three children, Henry, Edward and Beatrice. Edward migrated to South Dakota in America and bought a ranch. He wrote a number of books including *Rhymes of a Rancher* and *Daddams Book of Unatural History*. His sister married Charles Wingfield, descendant of the third son of the fourth Lord Powerscourt.

The house was acquired by Wellington Darley, a director of the Bank of Ireland. He was also associated with a variety of philanthropic causes, including animal welfare. The Darley family lost two sons and a daughter in the First World War. Arthur was on the HMS *Good Hope* when the ship was sunk in November 1914. Stella was a nurse and she was killed in 1917, while John, an officer with the 4th Hussars, was killed in 1918. The house was rented by the actor Sean Connery when he was filming at Ardmore Studios. The estate was broken up into sub-lots and sold in the late 1970s. Today two housing estates, Richmond Park and Ashton Wood, occupy the main grounds of the old Violet Hill estate. The original house still stands but the out-buildings have been converted into residential properties. The main house was sold in 2015.

LISLEE

William Shaw was born in County Tyrone in 1823 to Samuel Shaw, a church minister. William studied in Trinity College and moved to Cork, where he married Charlotte Clear, the daughter of a wealthy Cork merchant. Instead of a career as a church minister, William Shaw turned to politics and was elected as a Liberal Member of Parliament for Lislee near Bandon in County Cork. William was to become chairman of the Home Rule Party, only to give way to Charles Stewart Parnell. William Shaw did not contest the general election in 1885; in just a few months he would be declared bankrupt with the collapse of the Munster Bank, of which he was director. The Munster Bank was taken over by the Leinster Bank. William, as a ruined politician and banker, turned to journalism, writing for a number of newspapers and journals of banking affairs.

Today we are familiar with the phrase 'banking crisis' but in Ireland in the early 1800s there was a collapse of banks, including Newcomen's Bank, Alexander's Bank, and John Sadlier's Bank, which brought about the Bank of Ireland Restrictions Act of 1821, to ensure no other bank would fail. But in 1885 the Munster Bank collapsed and it was discovered that William Shaw had given himself a generous payment. The payment was described in *The New York Times* as 'plain fraud'.

In 1867 Shaw's Bank was taken over by the Royal Bank of Ireland, leaving William Shaw free to get involved in new ventures. He was drawn towards a new bank, the Munster Bank, that was established in 1864 and became its chairman. Due to mismanagement and bad decisions the bank found itself in financial difficulties. With mounting debts, the bank was liquidated in 1885. The Munster Bank was acquired by the Leinster Bank and adopted the title of the Munster & Leinster Bank. In 1966 the Mustster & Leinster and a number of smaller banks joined forces to form the Allied Irish Bank, one of the main banks in Ireland today.

William's wife, Charlotte died in London in 1868, so William came to live with his sister, Catherine Jane (Katie), at Lislee in Enniskerry village. Catherine died in August 1895, and William died in September 1895, both are buried in St Patrick's graveyard in Enniskerry.

SAN SOUCI/BRAY HEAD HOUSE

If you travel down the coastline by boat from Dublin to Wicklow there is one house that immediately stands out and catches you eye, 'San Souci', now Loreto Convent.

This building, painted white with a balustrade roof, is stunning. You can see why Mr Putland had a magnificent house built in 1811 on the Rock of Bray. Charles Putland was a keen sailor and owned his own yacht, *Enid*. The family wealth had come a long way from George Putland who arrived in Dublin from England as a blacksmith and metal worker in the mid-1600s.

Each generation developed the family wealth by getting involved in banking and property speculation. They purchased land at Dunshaughlin, County Meath, and in the counties of Kilkenny, Cork and Wicklow.

They first bought 500 acres at Woodbridge and undertook mineral exploration. Their Dublin home was located in Lower Mount Street.

The Putlands also invested money in the tea plantations of Ceylon, this is why the Putland coat of arms contains an elephant. Their circle of friends included Jonathan Swift, Daniel O'Connell and the educationalist, Dr Sheridan, and they became active members of the Royal Dublin Society. By the mid-1700s John Putland was devoted to public service, becoming High Sheriff of Dublin and Wicklow.

John married Catherine Moore in 1738 and they had eleven children including George, who was born in 1745 and was to inherit the property portfolio at Bray. The site now occupied by Loreto Convent was known as 'The Rock' and 'Hawksview'; the name 'San Souci' was first used about 1811, when the building of the mansion begun, but the first lease on the Bray property dates from 1771. The Putlands bought up adjoining lands in the mid-1800s and by 1820 they had amassed close to 100 acres from an initial lot of 16 acres.

George died in 1811, before the house was completed, and the property passed to his son, Charles, born in 1785. The Putland family got involved in the affairs of the town; the family donated a cup for the winner of the Putland Stakes run on Bray Racecourse, located near the river. The also took an active part in promoting the Bray Sea Regatta.

Mrs Putland established a school for the poor of Bray. Charles' brother George carried out reconstruction work at San Souci in 1835 and added a metal conservatory, the ridge of which was decorated with elephants. Charles shared his time between Bray, Blarney, County Cork and Paris. He married Constance Massy. During the Great Famine Charles reduced the rent of his tenants by 25 per cent, and this got the approval of Daniel O'Connell. In 1835 Mr Putland's workmen were building a new gate pier onto his estate at Bray Esplanade when the workmen discovered a number of human remains. The Roman coins buried with the remains were given to Mr Putland. Both Charles and George Putland were members of the 'Hollow Sword Blade Company' a venture capital company, financing projects they deemed worthy.

In 1861, the Putland family opened up access to Bray Head and laid out the Newcourt Road as part of the improvements on their estate. Also in 1861, Charles woke up one morning to read his death notice in *The Times* newspaper, when in fact his younger brother, George, had died. It was October 1874, and over 2,500 attended George's funeral and burial in St Paul's graveyard, Bray.

Charles, who was born in 1813, sold San Souci to the Loreto Nuns in 1850 and Charles and his family moved to another house on a different part of his Bray estate called Bray Head House. The nuns also maintained the farm established by Mr Putland. Just beyond the grouse-shooting bridge on the estate, the nuns built a burial vault in the Spanish style, as the early nuns in the order came from Spain.

Charles Putland died in 1874 and was succeeded at Bray Head House by his grandson Charles Walter Nelligan a District Commissioner for the East African Protectorate. He died in 1910 and was succeeded by his brother, John George Nelligan, a retired Royal Navy Officer who held the property until 1917, when they sold Bray Head House to David Frame. In turn, Dave Frame, a founder of Hammond Lane Foundry, sold the house in 1920 to the Presentation Brothers. David Frame purchased Corke Abbey in Bray. The Presentation Brothers ran a small farm, a day school and a school for boarders. The junior school was built in 1924 and in 2015 this building was demolished. An extension was added to Bray Head House in 1962 and today this building is used for adult education. The Brothers built a new secondary school with a swimming pool in 1972. The building was used in September 1975 to hold a civic reception for Cearbhall O'Dalaigh, the fifth President of Ireland, who was born in the town in 1911. The 1972 building was demolished in 2013 to make way for a new secondary school.

Michael Mallin, who was executed in 1916, had a daughter, Maura, who was educated at Loreto Convent, as were Mary O'Rourke and Gemma Hussey, both of whom held the post of Minister of Education in various governments. Sean Fitzpatrick of the Anglo Irish Bank was educated by the Loreto nuns and then by the Presentation Brothers, he lived at Camaderry Road, Bray close to both schools.

ARDMORE

Since 1958, Ardmore House has been the home of the Irish film industry and known as 'Ardmore Studio'. The house, referred to as a palace, was built for Thomas Langlois LeFroy in 1861, at a cost of £2,000. Thomas had a flirtation with the writer, Jane Austen, but he died in 1869 and the house passed to his son, Anthony Langlois Lefroy, who added an extension to the house in 1876. Anthony was a judge and he died in 1891 and was buried in the family vault in Mount Jerome graveyard in Dublin. Living in Ardmore in 1876 was a Charles Lefroy, along with his friend, George Napier McMurdo, a clerk in the Commissioners of Irish Lights, who undertook to climb Mount Blanc in the Alps without the aid of guides.

In 1906 William Henry Oldum purchased Ardmore and in 1907 he added new stabling and farm buildings. The Oldum family are best known as one of the large milling families in Ireland. On the Bray property the Oldum family kept a prize-winning Aberdeen Angus and

Jersey herd. In 1947 the property passed to Major John Byng Paget, who wrote an interesting article about covering crops to protect them from rooks. The property was bought by Louis Elliman of the Rank Group, and one of the first directors of the studio was Emmet Dalton, a soldier in the Republican Army and a close associate of Michael Collins.

BALLYMORRIS

This area has been associated with four families – those of Joseph Strong Esq., Richard Herbert Graydon Esq., Victor Charles Le Fanu, and Rowland S. Healy.

Joseph Strong Esq. was from Glenamuck, County Dublin, and rented land at Ballymorris, located off the Boghall Road and the Killarney Road. Joseph Strong died in November 1853 and is buried in Kilgobbin graveyard, County Dublin. He is buried with his daughter Anne and two of his grandsons, Robert and Charles. His eldest daughter Elizabeth married Nicholas Ogle D'Olier, a farmer from Ballyman near Bray. When Nicholas died in 1835, she married George Sale Bedford, the third junior officer at the Treasury in Dublin Castle. Before Joseph Strong's death in 1853 the property passed to Richard Herbert Graydon, who split his time between Ballymorris and his daughter Jane's residence at Culymacullwdy, County Armagh. Richard served as a magistrate for County Wicklow and a Poor Law Guardian for the Rathdown Union. Fortunes turned for Richard in 1850 when the High Court of Chancery took a case against him, and in the affidavit he was described as a lunatic. He died at Spring Hill, Carlow, in June 1856.

Victor Charles Le Fanu (1865-1939) was next to hold the property and he was a farmer and estate agent for the Earl of Meath. A keen sportsman, Victor was capped eleven times as a rugby flanker between 1886 and 1892. He played five times against England and three times each against Scotland and Wales. He played his club rugby with Landsdowne.

The final owner of the house was Rowland S. Healy, who had worked with Indian Civil Service. He lived at Ballymorris with his wife, Nora, and their children, Elizabeth, John, Susan, Geoffrey and Michael. Rowland died in 1975. Ballymorris was regularly used for tractor- and horse-ploughing matches run by the Rathdown Ploughing Society. Nora Healy died in 2013, aged 92 years.

ROYAL HOTEL BRAY

There has been a hotel on the site of the Royal Hotel since 1776. It was originally known as the Meath Arms Hotel, owned by John Quinn Sr, who came from Galtrim, County Meath. His residence was in Bray, just off the Seapoint Road and John Quinn named it Galtrim House. When John Quinn Sr died the hotel passed to his eldest son, William, and to his brother, John, who expanded the hotel and made it a posting hotel, with stage coaches calling up to six times a day. The journey time to Dublin was two hours, even if you changed horses at Cabinteely and Galloping Green. John Quinn died in 1869, and over the next decade the hotel changed hands at least five times, buyers included Mr Hayes, who ran the Royal Marine Hotel in Dún Laoghaire, Mr Jesson, who owned the Grand Hotel in Malahide, and Mr Mulliott, who owned a hotel in Suffolk Street in Dublin. Adam Findlater, son of Alex Findlater, who founded a chain store suppling top-quality food products, was the owner of the Royal Hotel for five years. His brother-in-law, John McCurdy, redesigned the hotel. John had already designed

the Shelbourne Hotel in Dublin. For the next thirty years Arthur Odell was general manager of the hotel.

In 1975, the hotel was sold as the Royal Starlight Hotel after extensive work had been carried out in 1973.

Many actors of the silver screen have stayed at the hotel, for example, Stan Laurel, Richard Greene, James Cagney, and Peter O'Toole. Other notables to stay at the hotel include King George IV, Percy Bysshe Shelley, Arthur Conan Doyle and Charles Dickens.

INTERNATIONAL HOTEL

This was built for Mr John Brennan in 1862 at a cost of £24,000, and it opened to the public in 1865. The adjoining road was called Adelaide, after his daughter. In the First World War the hotel served as a hospital, run jointly by the Red Cross and St John Ambulance. The hotel was renamed the Princess Patricia Hospital for Limbless Soldiers. The soldiers were donated Christmas gifts in December 1915. Gifts included cigarettes, cigars, vegetables, mince-meat, venison, turkeys, eggs, apples, oranges, flowers, evergreens, crackers, mince pies and plum puddings. Clothes were also donated with the Bray Women's Work for Wounded Soldiers, giving 389 shirts, 373 pairs of socks knitted, and 25 belts, a total of 767 articles in eight weeks.

After the war the hotel reopened, and during the Second World War it was occupied by the Free State soldiers and used as temporary hospital. The hotel built up a tourist trade during the 1950s, '60s and early '70s. In June 1974, disaster struck when the building was engulfed in fire. The site lay dormant for a number of years before it was occupied by Bray Bowl and Leisure complex.

CHRISTMAS WEEK 1915 IN
PRINCESS PATRICIA HOSPITAL

The soldiers and sailors in the Princess Patricia Hospital were given a turkey dinner at 2 p.m. served with potatoes, vegetables, copious amounts of plum pudding, mince pies and fruit. Mrs Majorie Bethel dressed up as a Red Cross nurse and gave each patient in the hospital a cigar and a box of matches. After lunch, everyone adjourned to the day room and Father Christmas arrived with a fanfare played by the local Boy Scout troop. There was a gift for everyone. Mr Mac Dermott, the owner of the Picture House in the town entertained the soldiers with several songs and dance routines. Between Christmas and the New Year

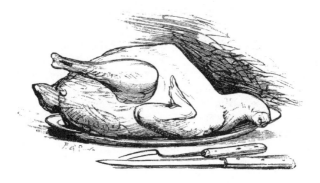

the soldiers and sailors enjoyed a variety of entertainment, including Mr Presto who performed conjuring tricks, dancing by local children, and, best of all, a Whist Drive with many prizes.

BRAY HEAD HOTEL

The Bray Head Hotel was built for J.F. Lacey in 1862. The Hotel has an interesting story regarding Mrs Lacey. Each week, two priests from Mount Argus in Dublin visited the Bray Head Hotel for lunch. One was Brother Charles, who was later beatified by the Catholic Church. A young boy by the name of John Patterson, at six years of age, was blinded after been hit in the eye by a stone. His parents brought him to Brother Charles in Mount Argus, who blessed him, and on his return home the boy was able to see the cattle in the field.

Brother Charles died in 1893, aged 71 and he was buried in Mount Argus. A case for his beatification and canonization was introduced in 1935. His coffin was exhumed in 1937 and a crypt was built in Mount Argus. The brothers went looking for the rosary beads he was given at the time he was ordained. It then transpired that he had given them to Mrs Lacey of Bray Head Hotel, who had died in 1929 and was buried in St Peter's graveyard in Little Bray. Before Mrs Lacy's death she passed the beads on to her cousin, John Byrne, who in turn bequeathed the beads to his daughter. The priest of Mount Argus offered Mrs Byrne a piece of Brother Charles' coffin in exchange for the rosary beads. In 1988, Pope John Paul II proclaimed that Fr Charles of Mount Argus was to be known as Blessed Charles of Mount Argus.

STRAND HOTEL BRAY

This was built for Dr Sir William Wilde, the father of Oscar Wilde. The building was known as Elsinore House. William Wilde was an eminent eye and ear surgeon but in 1864 his reputation was threatened when Mary Travers claimed that he had tried to seducer her in his Dublin Clinic. Mary set out her claim on a leaflet and dropped the leaflets into to the houses adjoining Sir William Wilde on Bray Strand Road and at Merion Square in Dublin. In response, Lady Wilde took Mary Travers to court, claiming in Bray Petty Session Court that Travers had defamed her husband in the leaflets.

KILLARNEY WOOD/ BROOK HOUSE SCHOOL

In 1860 Killarney Wood House on the Herbert Road was built for Judge David Richard Pigot as a summer residence. David was vice president of the society for the preservation and publication of the melodies of Ireland and held regular musical nights in the house. His son John was one of the first governors of the National Gallery of Ireland. His son David was master of the Four Courts and his youngest son Thomas was an architect.

In 1878 the house was bought by James Pim, a Dublin stockbroker and secretary of the Dublin & Kingstown Railway Company. James' son, Sir Alan William Pim, was one of the founders of the charity Oxfam. In 1892 the Pim family sold Killarmey Wood House to Adam Millar a, a wine and spirit merchant in Dublin. The Millar family farmed the 34 acres around the house. In 1927 they sold the house and land to the Co-operative Holiday Association who use the house as a guest house for paying guests and members of the association. In 1964 the Co-operative Holiday Association was renamed as the Countryside Holiday Association. The new association decided to reduce its property portfolio and Killarney Wood House was sold in 1972 to Brook House School, a private school. In 2012 Brook House School sold some of the land to Cairn Hill Nursing Home and a retirement/ nursing home was built in 2013.

5

CHURCHES AND SCHOOLS

NEW SCHOOLS OF THE 1800S

At the turn of the 1800s, and prior to the Education Act of 1830, a number of junior infant schools began to emerge in the Bray and Enniskerry area. Many of these schools were under the patronage of the wives of the local gentry. Harmony School near Tinnahinch Bridge was under the patronage of Lady Rathdowne and Mrs Grattan. The Enniskerry School and the two-room school house at Annicrevy were under the guidance of Lady Powerscourt. The Annicrevy school was built in 1816 and had a roll of 140 children. The master, Mr Cranston, was paid by the Education Board £15 per annum. The Enniskerry School was started a year earlier, in 1815, making it one of the oldest junior schools in the country.

The number of husband-and-wife partnerships as school teachers is evident in the census returns for 1901 and 1911. Thomas Sheedy and his wife Catherine were teachers in Curtlestown for many years in the early 1900s. Alice and Christopher O'Rourke did the same thing in Enniskerry National School, and in Enniskerry Parish School, Percy and Bertha Steede formed another partnership. The lane between Mr Steed's house and the School House in Enniskerry village is referred to by locals in Enniskerry as University Lane as the teacher held a university degree.

The school house at Ballyorney dates from 1825, as does the old school house at Curtlestown. The Wicklow Education Society, in its report for 1819, stated that the number of children educated in the parish of Bray was only 173. In 1821, the population of Bray was 2,029 and about a quarter of the population was of school-going age so we can deduce that about 300 children from Bray did not attend school. An Education Act in 1892 required children between the age of 6 and 14 to attend school. This act was updated in Ireland with the School Attendance Act in 1926.

NATIONAL SCHOOL
FOR ENNISKERRY, 1815

In 1815 the Viscountess Powerscourt started a school in the loft of one of the stables attached to Powerscourt House. This is one of the oldest schools in Ireland. The education provided was a model similar to that provided by Samuel Wilderspin, the famous English educationalist. In 1825 he paid a visit to Enniskerry. He praised the school for using his the teaching methods. In 1818, Lady Powerscourt moved the school from the loft at Powerscourt to a new two-room school in the village of Enniskerry. This school was used up to 2012, when a new school was erected near the main gate to Powerscourt House. Most of the rural schools in the district only had two rooms, one for the boys and one for the girls.

The school at Annacrevey was built in 1816, to cater for the children of the Glencree Valley. It was a two-room school. The teachers taught only reading, writing, and Latin. Religious education was confined to after-school on Saturday afternoons or at Sunday schools. There was an active Hibernian Bible Sunday School in the district. The Education Commission reports that the girls in the school were 'learning useful work'; this meant cooking, mending garments and knitting.

A POOR TEACHER IN 1823

A Traveller's Guide to Ireland, by Mary Grant, published in 1823, gives us a good insight into life in the Doujce Mountain area south of Powerscourt House.

'Near Doujce I came across a girl who lived by teaching the children of several families of the neighbourhood to read, going three months to one and then to another. The poor people were very kind to her. Her salary was not £4 a year, not sufficient even to cloth her.'

MRS PUTLAND'S SCHOOL

Mrs Putland's School, dating from the 1830s, was set up in Bray for children of the working class from the area. The children were both educated and clothed by the generosity of Mrs Putland. She employed one teacher who taught forty-two children. The school was supported by the sale of garments made by the children. Again, from reports of the Wicklow Education Society, we see that the vast majority of students were girls, making up thirty-six out of the forty-two on the roll.

MRS GRATTAN'S SCHOOL

When Henry Grattan died in 1820, Mrs Grattan turned her attention to the education of the children of the district of Newtown near Powerscourt. Mrs Grattan's son was one of the first Commissioners of the newly established National Education System introduced in 1830. Mrs Grattan's School had the wonderful name of 'The Harmony School'. The school had only one teacher, Miss Duffy. When Miss Duffy died the school did not reopen. A new National School was opened nearby in Ballyorney in 1825.

ST KEVIN'S INDUSTRIAL REFORM SCHOOL, GLENCREE, 1859

St Kevin's Industrial Reform School, Glencree (1859-1940) was the most westerly school in the district, 6 miles from Enniskerry (its telegram address was 'Enniskerry Six Miles'). It was located in the old military barracks, built in 1806, and had room for over 200 men and sixteen horses. The barracks was used to patrol the military road between Rathfarnham in County Dublin and Aughavangh in County Wicklow. With other barracks located at Drumgoff, Aughavanagh, and Glen of Immeall, the barracks at Glencree was closed in 1815 and was used as a military store until it was leased by Lord Powerscourt to the government to use as an Industrial Reform School, which was set up under the Irish Reformatory Schools Act of 1858. St Kevin's Reformatory School for Roman Catholic Boys at Glencree was run by the Oblate Fathers. St Kevin's was the first Roman Catholic Reform School established in Ireland on 12 April 1859.

Ireland had ten reform schools in the initial phase, and from the following table covering the period 1859 to 1871, we can see a rapid rise in the number of boys put into care. The boys could be put into care at the command of a judge, when the parents were not able to look after the boy. Most of the boys were committed following an appearance in the police courts for minor offences, and committal was for two to five years. Most of the boys spent five years in the reform school. By 1871 there was a total of thirty-two Industrial and Reform Schools on the island of Ireland.

Year	Number in Reform School
1859	140
1860	384
1861	539
1862	591
1863	606
1864	638
1865	642
1866	658
1867	662
1868	701
1869	787
1870	856
1871	970

An inspection of Reform Schools was carried out annually. According to the inspection report of St Kevin's of Glencree on 15 October 1871, the number of inmates was 324, nearly one third of all the students in Ireland. The inspectors found poor sanitary conditions, and during the year 1870 one boy had died of typhoid fever and since his death, sixty-one other boys had been stricken by the disease but had made a recovery. The inspectors reported that every precaution had been taken to avoid another outbreak, including destroying bedding and disinfecting the buildings. The cost of keeping a boy at the Glencree Reformatory was £23 1s per annum and payments made in 1871 amounted to £2,798 16s 8d.

The school was run by a manager, one clergyman, nineteen Oblate brothers, a bandmaster, a tailor, a carpenter, and four farm servants.

The inspectors found the buildings were in good repair and orderly, but overcrowded. The inspectors visited the chapel, the school room, the lavatory, the refectory, the bread store, the kitchen, the linen room, and the laundry. They noted that a new bake house had been constructed in 1870, and the boys were now instructed in baking by skilled artisans from Dublin. A new stone chapel has replaced a wooden structure erected in 1849 on a site given by Lord Powerscourt. One of the smaller dormitories had been fitted out as a hospital. A new three-storey building, 120ft in length, was built and used to house dormitories, a refectory, lavatories, schoolrooms, kitchen, bake-house, gashouse, laundry and workshops for the different trades.

During the year the farm of 120 acres was greatly improved and much additional ground had been fenced off and reclaimed from the mountain. The boys engaged on the farm were responsible for care of pigs, cattle, horses and sheep. The boys learned how to drain and reclaim land from the wild mountain, as well as the growing and harvesting of vegetables for use in the school. The boys also looked after the chickens and hens.

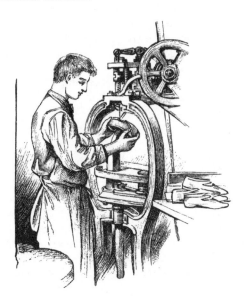

Industrial training was provided in cabinet making, woodcarving, woodturning, shoemaking, tailoring, stone-cutting, photography, and the manufacture of gas for the establishment. The school had a band and they gave concerts in Powerscourt House and in Dublin.

The manager pointed out that there was an additional cost in getting supplies delivered to Glencree. The suppliers of coal in Bray and Dublin charge an additional 10s for haulage of each ton of coal. He also reported that 230 boys had been discharged over the previous three years, 204 were doing well, three had since died, six were doubtful, seven had been convicted of other crimes and ten have been lost sight of.

Mr Éamon de Valera, who was both Taoiseach and Minister of Education, visited Glencree in November 1939, and made the decision to move the boys from Glencree to the reform school, St Conleth's at Daingean, County Offaly. The Daingean School was opened by the Oblate fathers in December 1870 and operated up to 1973. So, on 6 August 1940, the Garda transported 205 boys from Glencee to Daingean, with the Garda escort in civilian clothing. The mattresses and bedclothes were transported in large, open trucks on the same day. Fr Giancarlo had sought tarpaulin covers from the Garda to cover the trucks, but none was provided. The weather was typically Irish, with strong winds and fairly heavy, low clouds. This was at the same time as the Battle of Britain was taking place in the sky above. The residents of Glencree missed hearing the boys practising their musical instruments, and playing at garden parties hosted by Lord Powerscourt. Various visitors to Glencree, such at the Lord Mayor of Dublin, Alfie Byrne and Mr William Gladstone, commented on the playing skills of the boys and their musical repertoire.

The Glencree building remained empty until 1947, when the Irish Red Cross and the French Sisters of Charity used it for Operation Shamrock, when German and Polish orphans were housed in the old barracks.

GROWING VEGETABLE'S TO SUPPORT ENNISKERRY SCHOOL, 1896

The Powerscourt Cottage Garden Society and Industrial Society was established in 1882. The schoolmaster of Enniskerry, Mr Jeremiah Golden, gave evidence to the Education Commission in May 1897, and he said that he had been a teacher in Enniskerry since 1875. He was inspired by the ideas of the Powerscourt Cottage Garden Society as a way of introducing students to agriculture and a way of creating revenue for the school, as well as teaching students mathematics and other life skills. There was a spare parcel of land behind the school in Enniskerry village and it measured 1 rood and 20 perches. It was ideal for growing vegetables and in 1896 they produced the following from which they made almost £5 in profit for the school:

Produce grown	Profit
Potatoes	£1 15s 0d
Cabbages	£0 12s 0d
Onions	£0 15s 0d
Parsnips	£0 1s 4d
Carrots	£0 1s 0d
Celery	£0 4s 0d
Parsley	£0 2s 0d
Peas	£0 4s 0d
Cabbage Plants	£0 5s 6d
Turnips	£0 3s 6d
A total profit for the year 1896 was	£4 3s 4d

THE POWERSCOURT COTTAGE GARDEN SOCIETY AND INDUSTRIAL SOCIETY

The Powerscourt Cottage Garden Society and Industrial Society was formed in 1882, and held an annual show in the grounds of Powerscourt House. Lord Powerscourt put up the prizes and there was a special prize

for a window box display for houses in the village. No show was held in 1893, and the final show took place in 1902, just two years before the seventh Lord Powerscourt died. Admission to the show for parishioners of Powerscourt Parish was 6*d*, and children of the parish under 12 years paid 3*d*. All other adults paid 1*s* and children not from the parish were admitted at 6*d*.

NO SUMMER HOLIDAYS FOR BRAY SCHOOL

The Violet Hill boarding school near Bray, run by the principal Mr W. Hartshorn, opened in 1836. The school programme included instruction in the different branches of English education including geography, ancient and modern history, Latin, Greek and Hebrew, logic and mathematical sciences. Extras included French, German and Italian, music, drawing and dancing. Pleasant walks were organised through the demesne of Mr Putland to the shore at Bray. There were no summer vacations. The school moved from East Priory in Delgany to the bigger establishment at Violet Hill. The present Violet Hill house was constructed in 1868 for the Dublin barrister and Commissioner of the Friendly Societies in Ireland, Edward Lysaght Griffin. The new house had twelve bedrooms and a walled garden and the whole thing cost £5,000 while stables were added at a cost of £1,200. Griffin married Beatrice Cruddock and they had three children. Edward died in 1884 and left an estate of £53,931. The house has changed hands many times and been rented for short periods. The film actor Sean Connery lived at Violet Hill for a couple of months while he was filming *The First Great Train Robbery*, released in 1979.

THE FRENCH SCHOOL ON SIDMONTON ROAD

The French School in Bray was known locally as FSB, as this was the insignia on the girls' uniforms. The school opened in 1864 and operated until June 1966, in a red-bricked building at Numbers 1, 2 and 3 Sidmonton Place. The school was a private boarding school founded by a French woman, Heloise de Mailly, and a Miss Reilly. The school prepared girls for English state exams, the GCEs and the Cambridge Local Examinations. Up to the 1940s all subjects were taught in French.

The French School closed just two years after celebrating its centenary, a notice in the national newspapers stating that 'Due to the lack of financial support the Parents Committee has decided that it is not possible to save this long-established school.' The building was put up for sale in June 1966. The building was purchased by Joe Toner and rented to the Forestry Service. In 2000, the building was converted into luxury apartments.

ARAVON

Aravon School was originally located off the Novara Road, and spelling Novara backwards gives us Aravon. The school was established in 1862, and was originally called Bray College, 'a school for the sons of gentlemen'. The school was a merger of two private schools, one established by Mr Thomas Reginald Courteney at Fort View, Bray and another by Miss Haynes. The Bray College received boys from the age of 8. Mr Courteney, a classical scholar and gold medallist from Trinity College, announced in the papers that all the teachers at Bray College had university degrees. Miss Haynes took over as principal of Bray College in the 1870s, when Mr Courteney was appointed headmaster of Newport Incorporated School in County Tipperary, before he moved to Bandon Endowed School in County Cork in 1880. Bray College was renamed Aravon in 1894, and since then the school attracted the sons of gentlemen, many of whom were working overseas with the diplomatic service or with the military. The sons of Dublin merchants attended the college and some of the students achieved status after graduation, including Roger Casement, Chris de Burgh, and Louis Le Brocquy. In 1984, the school left the Meath Road and moved to Old Connaught.

ST PATRICK'S NATIONAL SCHOOL

The origin of St Patrick's National School goes back to 1892 when the building was constructed as the Meath Protestant Industrial School for Girls. At the breakout of the First World War the building was converted to a hospital. After some modifications the Duke of Connaught Auxiliary Hospital was opened to assist wounded soldiers and sailors who had lost a limb. After the war the building was acquired by the Drummond School, which moved from Chapelizod in Dublin. In 1944 it was bought by the Loreto Nuns who opened

St Patrick's National School, and added a number of extensions to the building. The facade of the building has not changed since it was built in 1892.

ST PHILOMENA'S

In 1896 the Religious Sisters of Charity, accepted an invite from the parish priest of Bray, Revd Dr Donnelly, to establish a community in the town. Five nuns took over a building on the Dublin Road known as 'Rack Rent House' on 15 August 1896.

The first five nuns in Bray spent their time looking after the community needs in the areas of health and clothing. There was an outbreak of cholera in the town the year the nuns arrived. The only school in the area was in the grounds of St Peter's church. The two-storey building taught boys on the first floor and girl's on the ground floor. In 1899, the teacher of the girl's school, Mrs McCann, retired, and Dr Donnelly asked the nuns to take over their education. As Rack Rent House was not suitable the nuns moved to Ravenswell House in April 1901. In the first year the nuns had 113 girls attending school, where, along with academic subjects the girls were taught hygiene and home skills such as cooking and mending. They were also taught singing. By 1904 the number of children on the roll was nearly 400. The nuns converted the old stables attached to Ravenswell House into classrooms. The nuns claimed they ran the biggest school in Bray, with average daily attendance at 70 per cent of those on the roll.

The nuns opened their doors to people affected by the flooding of the Dargle River in 1905. They would gather the children around the grotto of Our Lady in

May each year. The children would then march down Main Avenue to the gates of the convent, with the communion class at the head of the procession. The school buildings were extended in 1958, 1968 and 1979.

SUMBEAM HOUSE

Sumbeam House is one of the remarkable stories of Bray. It was founded in 1874 as a 'Cripples' Home' by Lucinda Sullivan, who was Lady Superintendent of Dublin's Adelaide Hospital, at the time. It was the first and only Cripples Home in Ireland and was entirely dependent on voluntary contributions. It was located on the Lower Dargle, beside the People's Park. Lucinda had decided to devote her life to helping the sick and disabled after being involved in a boating accident in Switzerland.

Disaster struck in August 1905 when the River Dargle burst its banks and flooded the Cripples' Home, destroying the basket-making room, school room, kitchen and dining room. The floor of the dining room gave way in the flood, causing damage to the new wing of the home, which had been built in 1876. The thirty-bedroom unit was destroyed, including the bedding and clothes.

The home had some high-profile visitors, including the Lord Lieutenant of Ireland Earl Cowper, Lord Mayor of Dublin Alfie Byrne, Prime Minister William Gladstone and, in 1897, the Duchess and Duke of York. The Queen of Roumania visited the home in 1890 and was presented with a box of 'White Wicklow Heather'. One of the patients, Gerald Palmer, was on the RMS *Leinster* in October 1918 when it was sunk by a German U-boat. Gerald lost his life, which was particularly poignant as he was heading to London to start a new life.

The home was renamed Sunbeam House in 1927. The home moved to a new Sumbeam House off the Vevay Road, and it is run by Sunbeam House Services (SHS), carrying on the work begun by Lucinda Sullivan and her followers.

BRAY NATIONAL SCHOOL

Bray National School began on the Seapoint Road and moved to the Little Flower Hall beside the Holy Redeemer church in 1880, and in 1932 it moved to a new school on the Vevay Road known as St Cronan's. The Vevay Road School was sold to a Gaelscoil in 1999 and St Cronan's moved to a more spacious building in the grounds of the

Loreto Convent. About six years ago an extension was added to the school to cater for growing demand.

ST PAUL'S SCHOOL

This was originally known as Bray Bridge School, in Castle Street in Bray. In 1904 the school moved to a new school called St Paul's on the Herbert Road, and in 1973 the school was demolished to make way for the first public car park in Bray. The school merged with St Andrew's and the two schools moved to a new building on the Newcourt Road. The building is shared with St Catherine's School, which caters for children with special needs.

ST PETER'S NATIONAL SCHOOL IN LITTLE BRAY

Built in the grounds of St Peter's church in 1864, the buildings are now used as the parish centre. In 1961 the school moved to a new building in the recently built Palermo Estate overlooking the former dog track in Bray.

GREAT CHURCH-BUILDING PROGRAMME 1858-1864

Within ten years of the railway coming to Bray, there was a great church-building programme, with six churches being built in the Bray and Enniskerry area between 1854 and 1863. The Presbyterian church of St Andrew's on Quinsboro Road kicked off the building programme with plans being drawn up in 1856. But in 1857 a new set of plans by William Joseph Barrewere were used, and building work began. The new church opened for worship on 12 September 1858. A new transept was commissioned in 1890, and a new porch was designed by Edwin Bradbury and Robert Edward Evens of Dublin in the early 1900s.

The Methodist church, also called St Andrew's, on the Ellington Road and Florence Road junction, was designed by Alfred Gresham Jones to replace an older church located near the Main Street. The new Methodist church was opened for worship in 1864. The final church in the great building programme in Bray was Christ Church, on Church Road. The foundation stone was laid in September 1861. St Paul's, the Church of Ireland parish church at the lower end of the Main Street, beside Bray Bridge, had served the parish since 1609, and was to become a chapel of ease when the new church was completed. The new church could accommodate 1,000 people and was built by T.H. Carroll. The church has a commanding location on the rock of Bray. The church was consecrated in July 1863, with the 174ft spire added in 1864 and, when William Gladstone visited Bray in 1877, he gave £5 towards a peel of bells for Christ Church. One of the curates of St Paul's in the 1840s, Henry Honywood D'Ombrain, was a keen rose grower. He became president of the Irish Rose Society and, on moving to England, president of the British Rose Society, this organisation is today known as the Royal Horticultural Society. In 1905, when Revd Henry Honywood D'Ombrain died in 1905, the Rose Society decided to name a rose after him. To mark the 150th anniversary of the Church in 2013, the Bray Cualann Historical Society, tracked down a hybrid of the Henry Honywood D'Ombrain rose and presented it to the church for its rose garden.

THE QUEEN OF PEACE CHURCH AND ITS LINKS WITH NAPOLEON III

The Queen of Peace church on the Putland Road also has a railway connection. The church was built in 1946 and a collection was made among the railway staff. The funds raised were used to purchase the Stations of the Cross, the sanctuary lamp and monstrance for the church. One of the striking features of the church is the painting hanging behind the main altar. The painting of 'Our Lady and St John at the Crucifixion' was a gift from Napoleon III to the Revd Miley, the president of the Irish College in Paris between 1849 and 1859. Revd Miley returned to Ireland and became parish priest of Bray. The painting hung in his home until 1946 when the then parish priest gave it to the new church. Revd Miley got a number of other paintings from Napoleon III, and these hang in St Peter's church in Little Bray, St Mary's church in Enniskerry, and the church of the Most Holy Redeemer in Bray, forming a common bond between the churches in Bray and Enniskerry.

ST PETER'S IN LITTLE BRAY

St Peter's in Little Bray was built in 1837 to replace a wooden church that was built near Crinken. St Peter's church will always be associated with Fr James Healy, who was born in Dublin in 1824 and was a Parish Priest in Little Bray from 1869 to 1894, before he moved to Ballybrack in July 1894 and died shortly afterwards. While in Bray he was so liked by all of the community that he would be invited to dine with lords of the manors, judges, and, if there was a social gathering Fr Healy would be there because he was famed for his wit. His memoirs were published in 1899 and is a great social history of Bray and Enniskerry.

St Peter's School was built in 1864 in the church grounds, and behind the church was the old graveyard, opened in 1842. Beside the graveyard is a large Celtic cross which was brought from the old church at Crinken. In 1905 additional ground was opened up for a new graveyard, and this was extended in 1954. Many in the graveyard are buried with the assistance of the Bray Tontine Society, later called St Kevin's Tontine Society, established in 1863. Buried in the graveyards are Fran O'Toole of the Miami Showband, who was killed in 1975, James Joyce's sister, Eileen Schaurek, Seamus Costello, and Edward Byrne, father of the broadcaster Gay Byrne. In the old graveyard there is a memorial to the Burke family; William, who was first librarian in Bray Public Library in 1911 and his son Captain E.J.(Paddy) Burke, who departed Atlin Airport in Canada bound for Laird Post in the Artic on 9 October 1930. On board with Paddy was Emil Kading, the mechanic, and a passenger, Bob Martin. The Junkers plane, belonging to Airland Manufacturing Company of Vancouver, had to cope with violent snow storms and strong winds that blew it off course. The plane encountered another snow storm, struck a hillside in low cloud and crashed. For the first few days they ate the provisions on board the plane, and also a caribou that they caught. After two weeks Paddy left his two passengers with the plane and he set off for a town called Fairchild. Fifteen days after the search had begun, a search party found the plane on 24 November 1930. Kading and Martin were still alive, and were taken back to Atlin. The search continued for six days and Paddy's body was discovered on 30 November 1930, just ten miles from Fairchild. He was buried in Atlin and his name was engraved on the family headstone in Bray.

ST FERGAL'S CHURCH

A temporary church on the Boghall Road was built in 1973, and the Archbishop Ryan of Dublin constituted St Fergal's parish in 1976. The church has links with the town of Wurzburg in Germany because St Fergal, an Irish missionary, became Bishop of Salzburg in 767. In 1979 Pope John Paul II blessed the foundation stone of the church during his visit to Maynooth. From 1973 to 2000 St Fergal's parish was under the care of the Franciscan Order, and since 2000 the parish has been

administered by diocesan priests. The town of Bray is also twined with Wurzburg in Germany, Begles near Bordeaux in France, and Dublin, California in the USA.

NEW CHURCHES IN BRAY

Over the years new religious groups have established churches and places of worship in Bray. The Coptic church on the Herbert Road uses an old television studio that was run by Bill Stapelton called 'Silverpines', across the road from Ardmore Studio.

LADY POWERSCOURT'S LINKS WITH PLYMOUTH BRETHERN

In 1845 the Revd Robert Daly, rector of Powerscourt, published the 'Letters and Papers of the late Theodosia A. Viscountess Powerscourt'. The letters are mainly to Revd John Nelson Darby, the rector of Calary church on the road between Enniskerry and Roundwood. The letters are written as Psalms but are actually love letters. Theodosia Anne Howard was born in 1800, the daughter of Hugh Howard and Catherine Bligh. Theodosia married the fifth Viscount Powerscourt Richard Wingfield. He was born in 1790 and in 1813 married Frances Theodosia Jocelyn, she died in 1820 and he married Theodosia Howard in August 1822. Within a year the Viscount was dead and the Viscountess devoted the rest of her life to acts of kindness.

Between 1831 and 1833 she held the Powerscourt Conference, an annual meeting of Bible students. The Conference was run by the Revd John Nelson Darby. Lady Powerscourt built a prayer meeting room at Brighton Terrace, Bray. She granted the Revd Darby the use of Powerscourt for prayer meetings. Lady Powerscourt died in 1836 and her letters were published in 1845. The Revd John Nelson Darby was ordained a deacon in 1825, and in 1826 was appointed to Delgany parish. From 1826 he served the people of Delgany and Calary. With the help of Lady Powerscourt he founded the Plymouth Brethren. He died in 1881.

6

WORK

MINING

One quarter of the population of County Wicklow was engaged in mining at its peak in 1870. Just north of the Ballyman Road, between Bray and Enniskerry, is Catty Gollagher Mountain, and on the northern slope of Catty Gollagher stands a smelting chimney and flue that comes from Ballycorus lead mining works just below. The Lead Mining Company of Ireland opened the Ballycorus smelting works in 1824, its total outlay was £1,025. They took ore from the foot of the hill of Ballycorus, as well as Luganure Mine near Glendalough. Ore was transported from a mine near Kildrum near Lifford, County Donegal. In 1844 Sir Robert Kane, the inspector of mines in Ireland, reported that there were two veins of lead in the Ballycorus mine of medium to good quality. Prior to 1836 there was a smaller flue beside the smelting works in Ballycorus. It was decided to build a chimney on Catty Gollagher; and the new chimney and flue cost the mining company about £10,000. The flue is over a mile long and is tall enough for a man to walk upright and there are several doors at intervals for the removal of deposits. The mine closed down in 1913. The chimney was so important to coastal navigation that it was inserted on Admiralty Charts after 1836.

BRAY ELECTRIC LIGHT WORKS

In 1896 the Bray Town Commissioners undertook to provide electricity for the town of Bray. The head fitter was Mr Christopher Coates, who was born in 1865. In 1885 he began working for the railway company and remained with the railway until 1890. He was employed by the Bray Town Commissioners in 1890, and in 1895 was assigned to Bray Electric Works. Mr Coates lived in Ardee Street and in 1911 he moved to a new house close to his work in Mill Lane. He lived there with his wife and daughter Christine. Disaster struck on Wednesday 10 July 1912, when a diesel engine exploded, killing Mr Coates and injuring Mr Souter, the chief engineer and Mr McDonald, the assistant engineer. Mr Souter lost both legs and Mr McDonald had head and face injuries. They were given medical assistance by Dr Raverty, who heard the explosion while working in his dispensary close by. The Town Commissioners and the board of trade carried out a report on the explosion. The factory clock stopped at 10.51 a.m., so the members of the Board of Trade were able to give an exact time of the accident. Mr Coates was buried in St Peter's graveyard in Little Bray.

FARMING

Between 1860 and 30 March 1880 County Wicklow sought loans under the Lands Improvements Acts, following the famine. There was demand for public works projects to alleviate the distress caused by the famine. The county sought a total of 186 loans. The amount issued to County Wicklow by the local government was £98,226 or 2.7 per cent of the total allocation of £3,117,187. These loans were given for drainage, farm buildings, labourer's cottages and mills.

Three County Wicklow landowners received the bulk of the grants: Lord Crofton, Lord Devonshire and Lord Powerscourt. In the 1840s the saw mill was constructed in the paddocks on Lord Powerscourt estate, and in 1860 a new dam was installed for the saw mill.

In 1870 Lord Powerscourt stated that his annual average rent received for the past three years was £20,000 and that he had spent between £1,600 and £1,800 on improvements to labourer's cottages.

In November 1883 the following townlands in the Powerscourt Estate were declared to be infected with foot and mouth disease; Cloon, Curtlestown Upper, Tonygarrow and Barnamire.

In the *Wicklow Newsletter* of 4 February 1888, Lord Powerscourt replied to allegations of mistreatment. He stated that he was planting some trees in the Ballyross area on the farm of Mrs Williams. It was not good land and he had reduced the rent accordingly when Mrs Williams' husband had died from an accident in a stone quarry. He had helped the family with seeds, oats and seed potatoes free of charge. He had also given them gifts of clothing. Mrs Williams had fallen behind with the rent, although it had been halved in recent years. The amount outstanding was £25 8*s* 4*d* in September 1887, and he had to begin legal proceedings to recover the rent outstanding.

In spring 1919, some 35,000 farmhands downed tools in a national strike. Lord Powerscourt used an eviction threat to get his men back to work. In 1923, most of Lord Powerscourt's tenants acquired their holdings in the land transfer under the terms of the Land Commission.

In 1932 Lord Powerscourt put the estate up for sale. The estate embraced some 2,000 acres, of these 700 comprised the estate proper, 1,000 more acres were moor and mountain, and the remaining 300 acres were good for tillage and grazing.

The average farm wage in Powerscourt in 1961 was £5 per week, and by 1982 was £80 per week.

SOLUS LIGHT BULBS

One of the main industries in the town was Solus Teo, the primary producer of electric light bulbs since 1935. The factory was opened by Count John McCormack, Ireland's best known tenor singer.

Solus made over 2,000 different types of bulbs, from 40 watts to 150 watts. The firm's range of lamps included miniature candle lamps for churches, photographic bulbs, car lamps, lamps for radio dials, bulbs for torches, reflector lamps for shop window display, special lamps for neon displays, and a wide range of domestic lamps. The average life-span of the lamps was 5,000 hours.

Solus also manufactured mercury discharge (colour-corrected) lamps used for street lighting. These were also used in factories and boxing stadiums. In November 1957 Solus sent a large consignment of light bulbs to America to specific standards. Solus made the lamps used in all traffic signals in Dublin.

Solus produced a lamp with the nickname 'Glamour Lamp', this lamp was sprayed with a silica powder to give it a pink lustre. This lamp was used in theatrical venues and in the dressing rooms of the stars of stage and screen. At peak production Solus Teo, employed 850 staff, mainly female.

Solus was one of the first companies to introduce recycling. If customers returned one dozen used lightbulbs, they were rewarded with 2*d*. If they returned the base with filament, they were rewarded with 3*d* per dozen returned. The returns could be sent to the factory at Corke Abbey or the company's showrooms at 14 St Andrew's Street, Dublin. In June 1984, Solus Teo went into receivership and it was bought by J. Garvey & Sons Ltd of Drogheda, who invested £1 million in new plant and machinery, and the new company Solus Lamps was established. The new company also had a plastics division called Nypro Plastics, making plastic components for telephones and other electrical devices.

PRINTING

Bray was the centre of printing in Ireland, with companies like Lithographic Universal, Dargle Press and Central Press producing high-quality journals and magazines. In 1972 a new industrial estate built on the Boghall Road saw two new printing companies set up in Bray. Industrial Print produced specialised labels for manufacturing companies in Ireland and worldwide. The second company was De La Rue Smurfit, producing high-quality security printing and cheque books.

Although the number of printing companies has fallen over the past half century with the growth of personal computers, the town has a number of printing companies producing high-quality material.

INDUSTRIAL YARNS

Industrial Yarns, manufacturing man-made fibres, was established in 1958 on the site of the old sand quarry at Ravenswell. When Industrial Yarns ceased production the offices and factory were converted into a furniture store and today the supermarket, Lidl, is based in the old Industrial Yarns complex.

FILMS

There are also two film studios in Bray. Silverpines was run by the late Bill Stapelton. He made television commercials and the studio doubled up as a recording for showbands. This studio is now a Coptic church.

On the Herbert Road in Bray is Ardmore Studio. The studio was opened by Taoiseach Sean Lemass in 1958, it was then owned by the Rank organisation, who made full length feature films and television series. The film studio changed hands a number of times. Films and television shows made at Ardmore include *The Blue Max*, *Johnney Nobody*, *The Spy Who*

Came in From the Cold, *The Lion in Winter*, *King Arthur*, *Of Human Bondage*, *My Left Foot*, *Vikings*, *The Tudors*, and *Penny Dreadful*. Many stars of the silver screen, including Eva Green, Daniel Day Lewis, Gabriel Byrne, George Peppard, Jimmy Cagney, Sean Connery, Peter O'Toole, Kim Novak, Robert Morley, Dame Angela Lansbury, Brenda Fricker, Donal McCann, Cyril Cusack, Harry Andrews, Elizabeth Taylor, Noel Purcell, Liam Neeson, Brendan Gleeson, and Robert Mitchum and have been filmed at various locations in Bray and Enniskerry.

ENNISKERRY

The main revenue for Enniskerry comes from tourism and agriculture. The village has a beautiful blacksmith's forge, built in 1859.

From the mid-1700s Ballybrew Quarry provided granite for the building of the gravening dock at Dublin Port. The quarry was acquired by John Sisks & Sons in 1954. In 1971 Ballybrew Quarries Ltd went into voluntary liquidation, and in 1973 the quarry was renamed Stone Developments Ltd. The company provided granite for many public buildings, including Pearse Street Garda Station in Dublin, the Central Bank in Dame Street, Dublin, Liberty Hall, Dublin, and the granite for the Railway Tunnel at Heathrow Airport, London. The quarry ceased production in 2005.

Enniskerry always had a small number of manufacturing industries. Forestry work was carried out by Powerscourt sawmill located in Powerscourt Deerpark, beside the Paddock Ponds on the slopes of Duoce Mountain. The sawmill provided employment up to the 1960s, producing wooden fencing, stake posts, and hurdles. In the 1860s, when a large oak tree fell on the Powerscourt estate, Lord Powerscourt had a table made from it at the sawmill.

In the village of Enniskerry the old garage of the Wicklow Hills Bus Company was acquired in the early 1960s by Pinnocks Manufacturing Co. (Ireland) Ltd, who had a smaller factory at Dartry Road in Dublin, making garments and sewing machines. In 1969 at High Court London, a petition was lodged for the compulsory winding up of Pinnock Finance Company (GB) Ltd and Pinnock's Factory at Enniskerry was put up for sale. The building was acquired by Fish Factory (KinTrack).

CLOTHING EMPIRE

In 1955 Donald Brooke Davies and his wife, Mary, set up a clothing company in the stable yard at Charleville House. Initially, they got a family called Farrell to produce woven shawls. The business took off, with garments of the finest hand-dyed Irish tweed, and lines designed by Donald and Mary. Their sons, Anthony, Richard and Mark did the marketing, while their daughter, Lucy, was a model for the clothing range. Lucy was a television production assistant with RTÉ and then with Thames TV.

In 1971, Lucy first married Sir Michael Edward Lindsay Hogg, a film director who directed *The Abbess of Crew* (1976). They divorced in 1978 and she married Anthony Armstrong-Jones, first Earl of Snowdon, who had separated from Princess Margaret Rose Windsor, sister of Queen Elizabeth.

The Donald Davies clothing company had outlets in Dublin, London, Paris, Tokyo and New York.

In the heyday of production 120 people were employed at Charleville and in Dublin.

The shop in the village of Enniskerry sold a wide range of tweed dresses and shirts produced on the Charleville Estate. The shop, known as Davies Enniskerry Ltd went into voluntary liquidation in March 1986.

Donald and Mary sold Charleville House in 1976 and returned to England to carry on farming.

The house was sold to Mr and Mrs Hawthorns, who lived in the house up to 1993, when it was sold to the property developer, Ken Rohan, and his wife, Brenda.

(KINTRACK LTD) FLAG ON ROCKALL

In November 1971, a bill was introduced in the House of Lords. The bill formally claimed for Britain the island of Rockall and the fishing and mineral rights around the island. The bill got its second reading in December 1971, and for over a decade there was a dispute over the ownership of the island between Ireland and Britain.

An advertisement was placed in the national newspapers on 13 June 1985 by P.D. Lane and Associates on behalf of Kintrack Fish Factory in Enniskerry. They sought permission from Donegal County Council to place a tricolour, flagpole and concrete base on Rockall Island.

Planning Applications
Co. Donegal – P.D. Lane and Associates. Permission sought from Donegal Co. Council by Kintrack Limited, Monastery Road, Enniskerry, Co. Wicklow, to erect an Irish Tricolour, a flagstaff and concrete base on Rockall Island. – M. Kenny.

POWERSCOURT FIRE

The Slazenger family were getting ready to open Powerscourt House to the public for the tourist season of 1975. A reception was held in the house on 3 November 1974, and a fire was lit in one of the rooms of the main house. In the early hours of 4 November 1974 the chimney caught fire and the resulting blaze destroyed most of Powerscourt House. There was a fear in the village that the tourism trade would suffer with such a loss, as the rebuilding of Powercourt House would cost millions. The house lay idle until it was re-roofed 1996. In 1997 the house was reopened to the public by President Mary Robinson.

Lord Powerscourt had opened up the gardens to the public in 1951. On Sundays the staff would guide the public around the gardens and armoury, which contained over 200 items of weaponry. In 1961, Lord Powerscourt sold the Powerscourt Estate to Mr Ralph Slazenger, chairperson of a sports equipment company. Mr & Mrs Slazenger were living at Durrow, County Laois when they sold the sports company to Dunlop and purchased Powerscourt. Their daughter, Wendy, married the tenth Lord Powerscourt in 1962. They were divorced in 1974. Powerscourt House is now run by the Slazenger Family Trust. The house and grounds were voted by National Geographic the third-best garden in the world. The estate now has two 18-hole golf courses. In 1932, Lady Powerscourt began to make a hand-woven rug measuring 28ft by 18ft. The rug had the Powerscourt coat of arms and was completed in March 1940. In 1997, Avoca Handweavers leased the ground floor of Powerscourt House selling clothing and household items. Powerscourt Estate runs the garden centre attached to the main Powerscourt House.

SPANISH HOLIDAYS

In the early 1960s there was the advent of package holidays to Spanish holiday resorts. Many of the tourists that came to Bray opted to head for Spain and other sunnier locations across the globe. Bray had been one of the places in Ireland that honeymooners headed for, it was also a destination for Dublin day trippers and the CIÉ Sea Breeze Excursions. Bray had set tourist weeks, and in the months of February, March and April, advertisements would appear in the British newspapers for apartments, chalets and rooms to let in Bray, on either full-board or half-board basis. The visitors came from the shipyards of Glasgow, the cotton mills in Lancashire, the car firms of Birmingham and the Midlands, and there were some Welsh visitors too. From the mid-1960s many of owners of large B&B houses and smaller hotels adapted to the changing times by converting the buildings into retirement homes or nursing homes. So, instead of tourists on their one- or two-week vacations between May and September, the owners of the B&B's and smaller hotels now had year-round clients.

Today there are a number of Language Training Schools in the area, and the students come from all over the globe. During the summer months large numbers of Spanish students arrive in Bray to learn English. So life has come full circle in Bray.

7

BRIDGES, STREETS AND MONUMENTS

CROSS ON BRAY HEAD

The cross on Bray Head is a modern landmark of Bray. The cross was erected to mark the Holy Year in 1950. It was paid for by the school children of Bray, who gathered up their pennies, and the concrete cross was erected by a local builder, Mr Dodd. The newspapers of 18 September 1950 carried reports of the blessing of the cross the previous day. But the blessing of 17 September 1950 had to be cancelled due to inclement weather. The cross was instead blessed on Sunday 23 September 1950, and the event was not covered in the newspapers.

ENNISKERRY BRIDGES

The Irish name for Enniskerry is 'Áth na Sceire' meaning the 'rocky ford'. No longer do you have to cross a ford at Enniskerry because it has two fine bridges over the Glencullen River, linking the village with the Dublin Road. In 1861, plans were drawn up by Mr Henry Brett, the Wicklow County Surveyor, to remove the iron bridge near the Powerscourt Arms Hotel and replace it with a stone structure. The new bridge was designed with a single arch and fine balustrades on either side to make the entrance to Enniskerry aesthetically attractive. The bridge was opened in September 1865, and the cost was shared by the Grand Jury and Lord Powerscourt. The upper bridge on the Knocksink Road, beside the Catholic church, was built in 1859 and was the highest road bridge in Ireland until the construction of the toll bridge over the M50.

THE BRIDGES AT BRAY

A four-arch Bray bridge was constructed in 1666, but this collapsed in 1741 and was replaced by a new bridge within the same year. The 1741 bridge was replaced in 1856 by a new three-arch bridge designed by Mr Henry Brett. The bridge was built by David Edge, and it bore his name. The bridge was renamed on 5 July 2015 in honour of the Bray resident Fran O'Toole, who was the lead singer with the Miami Showband. Three members of the showband were killed outside Newry in 1975, including Fran O'Toole.

The Railway Bridge downstream was built in 1853, a year prior to the opening of the railway between Bray and Dublin. The railway company had to narrow the channel of the river and build a small shipping dock. Between Bray Bridge and the Railway Bridge there was a wooden footbridge linking Ravenswell Road and the Seapoint Road, this bridge was built at the time of the railway coming to Bray. It was closed in 1870 and removed shortly afterwards. In 1905, James Whalley and Peter McCann appeared in court for poaching salmon on the Dargle River near Bray Bridge. They were observed by Constable McLoughlin and Mr William Dodd, clerk of the Conservators of the Fisheries. Mr Whaley was fined £4 and Mr McCann £2. The judge awarded Constable McLoughlin one third of the penalty because he was impeded in his duties.

On 5 June 1915 the District Inspector Molony of the police observed Mrs Mary Neill of Bray destroying a military poster at Bray Bridge. Mrs Neill was charged under the Defence of the Realm Act for tearing down the poster asking for '30,000 more men for Lord Kitchener's Army'. Mrs Neill's brother was in the army, in the Irish Brigade. Mrs Neill was bound to the peace and fined £5.

Bray Harbour Bridge was constructed in 1890, at the time the harbour was built. The bridge collapsed in 1980 and was replaced with a new bridge. The new bridge was named in honour of William Dargan.

SILVER BRIDGE

The original Silver Bridge was blown up in the civil war in 1923, and the new Silver Bridge was built in 1925, made of stone, with a silver hand rail. The bridge was on the old Dublin to Wexford Road and the scene of many crashes. Today, motorists pass the Silver Bridge on the N11 without even noticing it. In February 1981, three people were killed in a road accident at the bridge. In May 1988, two young ladies, Mrs Kavanagh and Miss Clarke, went out horse riding along the Dargle

River, a stretch of the river near Mrs Kavanagh's home. They did not return. A few days later, Mrs Kavanagh's body was found in a pool beside the Silver Bridge. The body of her friend, Miss Clarke, was never recovered. The Silver Bridge was also considered by poachers as the best spot on the river to catch salmon. In July 1964 the water bailiff, Mr John Kinsela, caught Mr James Byrne red-handed trying to spear a salmon. Mr Byrne was brought before the courts and was fined £12 and had to pay £5 in costs.

TOWN HALL AND MONUMENT IN BRAY

In 1879, Lord Meath decided he wanted to present the Bray Town Commissioners with a Market House, Town Hall and offices, at a cost of nearly £7,000. He maintained the right to hold six meetings a year in the Town Hall and also appoint the caretaker, but the Town Commissioners would pay the wages of the caretaker. Lord Meath's architect, Thomas Newenham Deane, designed a building derived from a coffee tavern and hostelry created by Ernest George and Harold Peto for Newark-on-Trent in Nottinghamshire. The Market House and Town Hall, in its mock Tudor style, is a wonderful building both inside and out. The stained-glass windows contain the coat of arms of all branches of the Brabazon family. In the council chamber there are four oak chimney pieces dedicated to Literature, Justice, Commerce and Agriculture, designed by J. Reynolds Smith. The foundation stone was laid in 1881, and by the end of 1883 the building was complete. There were a number of delays which frustrated both Lord and Lady Meath. In her diary, Mary Countess of Meath recalls her feelings on 24 January 1884, 'Off to Euston where I met Reg, and was very pleased to get him back again safe and sound from Ireland, where he had a dreadful time of it, what with the Bray Town Commissioners to whom he wants to hand over the Market House and Land Leaguers. They even threatened his life on Christmas Day. So much for gratitude amongst the poor, easily led Irish'. At the same time, Lord and Lady Meath donated the People's Park with Park Lodge to the Bray Town Commissioners. The items mentioned in Lady Meath's diary refer to delays in drawing up the lease by the Bray Town Commissioners, and the appointment of a competent gardener with a 'tidy wife' to occupy the lodge in the People's Park.

The lease was drawn up for the Town Hall in April 1884, and the Commissioners held their first meeting in the new Town Hall on 19 May 1884. The final costing of the Town Hall was £6,359 3s 9d, made up of building work (£5,366 7s 6d), fountain (£177 6s 6d), furniture

(£157 15s 0d), clock (£105 16s 0d), glass (£151 5s 0d), roads paid for by the Town Commissioners (£95 0s 7d) and architect's commission (£305 13s 2d).

The statue in front of the Town Hall has a wyvern mounted over four drinking fonts and at the base of the monument is a drinking trough for horses. The wyvern is the mythical creature featured on the Brabazon coat of arms. The Brabazon family ancestors came from Brandt in Belgium. The original architect's drawing was for a Norman knight, instead of a wyvern, mounted on the fountain. The Norman knight was to represent the ancestor of the Earl of Meath, known as Jacques Le Brabacon, the standard bearer of William the Conquer. In Bray, the wyvern is referred to as the devil. In 1990, the Town Hall and market place were in much need of repair, as was one wing of the wyvern. The Town Council, with a developer, refurbished the space behind the Town Hall, by the town fire service and the town pound, turning it into retail outlets. First a restaurant was opened in the historic Town Hall and when this failed, McDonald's took over the restaurant. The building was re-roofed and the interior and exterior of the building were painted. The town was granted Township status in 1866 and the table used for the first council meeting is the table in the council chamber in the Town Hall. The Town Hall was used as the Bray Heritage Centre from July 1985 to 1990, when the developer carried out the repairs.

DR THOMPSON MONUMENT

Standing outside the Royal Hotel on the Main Street is a memorial to a Bray medical doctor. Bray is the only town in Ireland with a memorial to a town medical doctor. Dr Christopher Thompson was born in Dublin in 1815, the son of a Dublin Rate Collector. At the age of 15 he entered Trinity College and on qualifying as a doctor joined the Royal Army Medical Corps and was assigned to the 43rd Light Infantry stationed in Queenstown (Cobh). He was promoted and moved with the Rifle Brigade to Aldershot and from there to Portsmouth General Hospital. He returned to Ireland in 1859 and lived at Fitzwilliam Square in Dublin, and at Duncairn Terrace in Bray. He married Jane Hopkins, the daughter of Dr William Hopkins. Dr Thompson fought an outbreak of cholera in the town in 1876 but he died of typhoid pneumonia in December of that year. A meeting was called in January 1877 and from subscriptions and donations the committee had enough funds to erect a memorial. Dr Thompson is buried in St Paul's graveyard, overlooking the memorial on Main Street. His wife, Jane, who died in 1888, is buried in Mount Jerome in Dublin, alongside he father.

BRAY BANDSTAND

Prior to 1908 Bray had three bandstands, a morning, an afternoon and evening one. The bandstands were wooden structures. When the Great Exhibition of Dublin, held in Herbert Park, finished in November 1907, the organisers sold off the pavilions, bandstands, cottages, and all other moveable fixtures. The buildings and fixtures were offered to town councils around Ireland. Bray decided to buy two second-hand bandstands to replace the afternoon and evening bandstands on the seafront. The evening bandstand came with a clock on the roof, but the Bray Town Commissioners decided they did not want the clock and they sold it to the Royal Dublin Society. The bandstands were erected on the Esplanade during the spring of 1908. The afternoon bandstand was opposite the Esplanade Hotel. In 1949, the Irish singer Val Doonican played on the bandstand. The evening bandstand was renamed the Grand Marine Bandstand, and a crowd of 4,000 gathered on 24 July 1908 to witness a fine musical performance from military bands and a selection of bands from Dublin. The evening concluded with a fireworks display.

The pillars of the bandstand were made by Hammond Lane. The person casting the company stamp on the base of the pillars must have had an off day. Instead of spelling Dublin, he cast 'Dubiln'. His error can still be seen on the bandstand. The afternoon bandstand was demolished in the early 1960s, leaving only one bandstand on Bray seafront.

From 1908 the railway company would carry bands and their equipment free of charge to Bray. The bands had their own dedicated followers whether they were playing in the People's Park in Blackrock, the pier in Dún Laoghaire, or on the seafront in Bray. Later, the bands hired buses to take them to the musical venues. Bands from Dublin included The Artane Boys Band, The Number 1 Army Band, the Garda Síochána Band, St James Brass and Reed Band, The Irish Transport Band, The City of Dublin Connolly Pipe Band, and the British Legion Band. The bands played from 4 p.m. to 6 p.m. and from 7 p.m. to 9 p.m. sometimes it was difficult to hear the bands, due to the noise of day trippers listening to their transistors and the big matches from Croke Park. During the summer months Guinness would place its musical clock beside the bandstands.

STREET NAMES

There is only one street in Enniskerry, from the Monument to Troy's Corner. The name given to this bit of road is **Front Street**. The street furniture on this stretch of road includes a water pump and the phone kiosk designed by Sir Giles Gilbert Scott, with unique-style eighteen-panel windows. This type of phone kiosk was first used in Ireland at the Eucharistic Congress in 1932, but very few remain in the towns or villages of Ireland. The phonebox has featured in a number of television commercials.

Bray, like other towns in Ireland, has roads called after townlands, 1916 leaders, trees, churches, convents, castles, other political figures, and, of course, Dublin Road. Some other roads have less obvious links.

Adelaide Road is called after the daughter of Mr John Brennan, who built the International Hotel on the Quinsboro Road.

Galtrim Road and **Quinsboro Road** are called after the Quin family who ran the Royal Hotel Bray. The family came from Galtrim, County Meath.

The **Herbert Road** is called after Lord Herbert Lea, a member of the Pembroke family and the area around the Herbert Road was part of the Pembroke Estates.

Adree Street in Little Bray was part of the artisan dwellings promoted by Lord and Lady Meath. The eldest son of Lord Meath is Baron Ardee.

Roads called after political figures include Connolly Square, Pearse Square, James Everett Park, Wolf Tone Square, Roger Casement Park, Parnell Road, and Davitt Road.

Maitland Street is called after Lady Mary Jane Maitland, the daughter of Thomas Maitland, 11th Earl of Lauderdale, and Amelia Young. She married Reginald Brabazon, 12th Earl of Meath, on 7 January 1868, and was styled the Countess of Meath in 1887. She died on 4 November 1918.

Meath Road is called after Lord Meath.

Putland Road is called after the Putland family. It was originally called the 'Road of Ten Houses' after the road was completed, as there were only ten houses at Sydenham Villas.

A number of roads are called after royalty. **Albert Avenue** is one of the roads leading off the seafront, the next road is **Victorian Avenue**, and completing the royal set is **King Edward Road**, built in 1910, off the Killarney Road.

Dargan Street is called after William Dargan, the railway engineer who brought the railway to Bray.

Edward Road, off the Putland Road, is called after Edward Dempsey, as the houses were built on the Dempsey Estate. The Dempsey family ran a family butchers shop on Main Street.

Camaderry Road is called after Camaderry Mountain near Glendalough.

Cuala Road is called after Cuala, an ancient name for the area of North Wicklow.

8

TRANSPORT AND COMMUNICATIONS

FAME AND VICTORY

On 29 October 1754, Lord Powerscourt accepted a wager of 2,000 gold coins from the Duke of Orleans, Lord Powerscourt would complete the journey from the Chateau at Fontainebleau to Les Gobelins in Paris, a distance of 42 miles in less than two hours. Lord Powerscourt could use three horses, but he decided to use his two horses, 'Fame' and 'Victory'. Lord Powerscourt set off at 7.10 a.m. and arrived in Les Gobelins in Paris at 8.47 a.m. To make sure there was no skulduggery en route, observers were placed every 27ft. The event was recorded by the artist Charles Germain Saint Aubin, and his drawing is part of the Rothschild Collection in Waddesdon Manor near Aylesbury in Buckinghamshire, England.

OLD MAIL COACH ROAD TO CARLOW

According to the *Post-Chaise Companion* of 1786, Enniskerry was on the alternative coach route from Dublin to Carlow. Strange as it may seem, after leaving Dublin a traveller would have passed Miltown, Churchtown, Kilternan, Enniskerry, Powerscourt, Rathdrum, Aghrim, Hacketstown, and Tullow, a distance of 49½ miles, with a journey time of eight hours. This allowed for the changing of horses at various coaching inns en route, including one at Tinnahinch, near Enniskerry. The Coaching Inn at Tinnahinch was to become the home of the Member of Parliament Henry Grattan in 1782.

THE TWO-PENNY POST

In 1826 Enniskerry was granted Two-Penny Post status prior to the first ever postage stamp being released, the famous Penny Black. The Penny Black was issued in 1840 and showed the head of the monarch Queen Victoria. The stamp showed that payment had been made for delivering the letter. Before the Penny Black, most letters were delivered by the postman, who asked for payment from the person receiving the letter. Changes in the way the Post Office charged for delivering letters meant that posting letters became much cheaper, and it made sense to ask people to buy a stamp, or label, as it was called at first, and stick it on their letters. These early stamps had to be cut out from a large sheet of 240 with a scissors and then glued onto the envelope. Local hotels became postal depots where a mail coach would stop and letters were exchanged. In most towns in Ireland there were two kinds of car, a standard omnibus and mail coach. The standard service that did not carry mail could be hailed by passers by.

BRAY CABMEN REFUSE TO TAKE A PASSENGER TO ENNISKERRY

A lady shareholder of the Dublin and Wicklow Railway Company wrote a formal complaint to the manager of the company. On her arrival in Bray on Sunday 19 June 1864 at noon, she called a cabman standing beside his vehicle, she asked him to take her to Enniskerry. The cabman said he was engaged and drove off with an empty carriage. She then hailed a second cabman, but he also drove off with an empty carriage. She looked around for a policeman, but none could be found. She had to hire a man with an open carriage to take her to Enniskerry. The weather on that day that was exceedingly rough and stormy. In 1870 the railway company established its own omnibus service to Enniskerry.

CYCLE POLO, 1891

There aren't many towns in Ireland can claim they invented an Olympic sport.

Ralph McCready represented Ireland in Cycle Polo in the London Olympics of 1908. On 23 July 1908 in Crystal Palace, before the King, Ireland played Germany in the demonstration sport of cycle polo. Ireland beat Germany 4:1. The sport was devised by Ralph's father, Richard J. McCready, at the Scalp near Enniskerry in 1891. One of the first people to play cycle polo was the song writer and artist, Percy French who was a personal friend of Richard J. McCready. Ralph went on to be Chief Medical officer of New Zealand. In 1958 he retired and moved to Chuckfield near Brighton, in England, where he died in 1968. Cycle polo is today played across the world.

BRAY CABMEN

At the turn of the twentieth century the Bray cabmen agreed the following rates for the carriage of passengers for 1901-2.

- Set down within the township minimum charge 6 pennies and maximum fare one shilling

- No fare outside the township to be less than 1 shilling.

- The Dargle, Powerscourt House and the Waterfall,

returning by the Rock Valley and Hollybrook, the whole distance of 14 miles (23km), for one or two persons 10 shillings, three or four persons 12 shillings.

- Lough Bray and back 26 miles (43km) 14 shillings for one and 16 shillings for two.

- Glencree Reformatory and back 22 miles (36Km) 12 shillings for one and 14 shillings for two.

Prices for 1901-1902.

SHORTEST TELEGRAM

For 163 years, up to 14 July 2013, a person could send a telegram. The record for sending the shortest telegram is held by Bray resident, Oscar Wilde. While in Paris he cabled his London publisher concerning his new book. Wilde wrote a question mark '?' on his telegram and his publishers replied with an exclamation mark '!'.

UP, UP AND AWAY

On Saturday 28 September 1912 at 3 p.m. Mr Valentine and three mechanics prepared a wooden aircraft for take-off from the lawns of Powerscourt House. Between 200 and 300 people were present. A priest stepped forward and gave Mr Valentine a blessing.

Due to the wind conditions the ascent was put off till 5 p.m. At 5 p.m. the plane took off and soared over Powerscourt House. The newspapers reported that Mr Valentine was in the air for about 10 minutes and achieved an altitude of 1,000ft. The crowd roared as the plane circled over Sugarloaf Mountain. As he descended onto to the lawn at Powerscourt the crowd waved handkerchiefs and threw their hats in the air.

RELIEF SHIP FOR BRAY

Within a week of the Easter Rising, many Dublin suppliers were unable to fill orders for Bray traders. On the suggestion of Fr Richard Colahan of Bray, Mr Magee the Chairman of the Urban Council called a meeting of the merchants in the township. A committee was formed and it was decided to organise relief provisions in the township by sending a boat to Liverpool. The boat was kindly lent by Mr Collier, a timber and coal merchant in the town.

The ship docked at Bray on Wednesday 3 May 1916. The consignment of provisions was worth £3,000 and the provisions went on sale in the town at normal prices. The vessel had to cross the Irish Sea during the height of the First World War, with every chance of hitting a mine or being attacked by German aircraft or U-boats. The consignment and ship were underwritten by Sir Stanley Cochrane, who lived at Woodbrook near Bray. He was a director of the drinks company Cantrell and Cochhrane.

THE BIRTH OF BUS ROUTES 44, 45, 45A

The 1920s and early 1930s saw the independent bus companies operate in a fierce competition, with the lives of passengers and other road users being put at risk. In Bray District Court in August 1931 the judge warned the Wicklow Hills Bus Company and St Ann's Bus Company about playing bus relay-races, following an accident on 27 June 1931 at the Scalp near Enniskerry. The St Ann's bus, driven by Francis Gunning, and the Wicklow Hills Bus, driven by James Kelly, collided. Mr John Rochford, a passenger on the Wicklow Hills Bus was injured. The judge at the Bray District Court ordered that Mr James Kelly pay 20 shillings and Mr Francis Gunning pay 40 shillings in fines.

In the 1920s the Dublin/Enniskerry route was serviced by the Residents Bus Company, which initially had two 16-seater Renault buses. The Resident Bus Company was replaced by the Wicklow Hills Bus Company, which began in 1927, and was owned by Mr Thomas Fitzpatrick, a Mullingar businessman. The Transport Act of 1933 saw the consolidation of independent bus companies, with the Dublin United Tramway Company and operators requiring a licence to operate on defined routes. The buyout of the independents in Dublin took a couple of years and cost the Dublin United Tramway Company £448,428.

The Wicklow Hills Bus Company ceased running at Easter 1936, and the route between Enniskerry and Dublin was assigned number 44 Bus route in the Dublin Tramway Company network. The St Kevin's bus service remained as an independent operator offering a daily service to Dublin from Glendalough.

All other independent-operated routes were taken over by railway companies or the Dublin United Tramway Company. The bus route from Enniskerry to Bray railway station was granted to the Great Southern Railway Company. Although the railway between Dublin and Bray was operated by the Dublin and South Eastern Railway Company, it became part of Córas Iompair Éireann (Irish Rail) in 1945.

The St Kevin's bus service was established in 1927, operating from Glendalough and Dublin, and is one of the private operators still driving the same route that they did in 1927.

TRAVEL TO DUBLIN FOR WORK

A travel survey in 1970 estimated that 2,000 commuters per day travelled from Bray, Enniskerry and Greystones to Dublin for work. Another survey taken in the year 2000 stated that the number of commuters had risen to 4,000 per day from the towns of North Wicklow.

SETTING FIRE TO A BUS

Cornelius Buckley, a motor mechanic of Enniskerry, was charged at Bray District Court on 19 September 1931 for setting fire to a bus valued at £400, which was the property of Mr Thomas Fitzpatrick, the director and owner of Local Services Ltd. The incident happened at Kilcroney on 12 September 1931, just after midnight. Mr Buckley, an employee of Local Services Ltd, was returned for trial to the Circuit Court.

HOT WORDS IN BRAY BUS

A newspaper article with three banner titles – 'Hot words in Bray Bus', 'Where courtesy is lacking' and 'Woman summoned for assault' – tells us an interesting story of a Bray bus in March 1928.

Before Mr Justice Reddin in Bray Court was conductor, Mr James Murray of Washington Villas, Dargle Road, Bray and Mrs Marita Roper of 'Fona', Old Connaught Avenue, Bray.

Mr Murray was described as an old tram conductor who was celebrated for his wit and courtesy. On 18 March 1938 Mrs Roper got on his bus at Old Connaught Avenue and handed him a penny, and he punched a penny ticket. When the bus arrived at Woodbrook, the end of the stage, he told the lady to either pay the excess, get off the bus, or else give her name and address. She went to the back of the bus and tried to get off, while the bus was travelling at thirty miles an hour. Murray put his arm across the door and then Mrs Roper struck him twice in the face. She also tried to bang the bell of the bus a number of times.

Mrs Roper said the conductor was very rude. They had argued when she boarded the bus. The conductor claimed she had got on at Sunnybank. She replied that she had got on at Old Connaught Avenue and her destination was Crinken. She had made this journey for the past six years and the fare was one penny. At Crinken she sprang to her feet and banged on the bell of the bus. When the conductor would not let her off, she hit him in the face.

When the bus stopped in Shankill, she walked to the Guards Barracks and made a complaint about the conductor. Her hand and arm were bruised.

Mr Tyrell, a solicitor, appeared for Mr Murray, and stated that the conductor might have been dismissed, save only for the action of his union.

Mrs Roper expressed regret for what had happened and Mr Justice Reddin applied the Probation Act, but ordered her to pay one guinea costs.

A cross summons by Mrs Roper against Mr Murray was dismissed.

LAST TRAIN FROM HARCOURT STREET

In 1958, a report on the closure of railways was presented to the Board of Córas Iompair Éireann, and it decided to close or curtail a number of railway lines. The railway line between Bray and Harcourt Street was selected for closure, and in 1959 the final train ran between Harcourt Street and Bray.

The railway was taken up. The Luas line now runs on some of the existing track bed.

QUINSBORO ROAD UNDERPASS

In 1880, the Board of Trade was asked to examine an underpass that would link the Quinsboro Road and Bray Seafront. The railway company had twenty-eight trains a day passing in each direction at the level crossing at Bray, causing delays each time the gates had to be shut. The railway company had inserted a pedestrian companion gate beside the level crossing to aid invalids, and had placed a footbridge

for the more able bodied. The plans for the underpass were drawn up, but were not implemented.

ENNISKERRY RAILWAY

This is best described as the railway that never ran a locomotive. The Bray and Enniskerry Railway Company was established by an Act of Parliament in 1866. Because the work was not completed, the railway company had to get additional acts passed in 1894, 1897 and 1900. The company built bridges, embankments, widened roads and laid the track bed and rails but they ran into financial difficulties in 1903, and before the first train ran the rails were lifted and sold off. A local historian, Liam Clare, has published a book, *Bray & Enniskerry Railway Company* (Nonsuch, 2007), on the rise and demise of the railway.

PROPOSED TRAIN FROM BRAY TO GLENDALOUGH

In the 1870s, when railways were a fashionable investment, a number of investors saw the potential of visitors coming to the religious site of Glendalough. The plan was to create a light railway line between Bray and Glendalough. The proposed route was along the Quinsboro Road, onto the Main Street in Bray, the route would pass Kilmacanogue,

Newtownmountkennedy, Roundwood, and Laragh and arrive close to the Royal Hotel in Glendalough. The Dublin to Blessington line would be extended to Glendalough. So tourists could make a round journey of the Wicklow Hills. The Bray to Glendalough Light Railway only got as far as the planning stage.

BRAY BOAT RACES

On 7 September 1872, Mr P. Mc Swiney of Bray announced that boat races would take place at Bray seafront. The rowing races on 10 September 1872 included crews made up of amateurs, fishermen and coastguards. Military bands played while the races took place. The evening concluded with a grand fireworks display.

THE PLIGHT OF BRAY FISHERMEN

A meeting of the fishermen of Bray was held on 23 August 1888, in the Esplanade Baths.

The Revd Charles Cuddihy of Enniskerry chaired the meeting. Before them were two resolutions.

The first resolution was to thank the gentlemen of Bray who gave subscriptions for the repair of the boat slip, and the Dublin & Wicklow and Wexford Railway Company, who provided some iron rails. This resolution was proposed by Mr John Devitt and seconded by Mr Thomas Byrne.

The second resolution that the Bray Town Commissioners might take steps to construct a harbour. This resolution was proposed by Mr Valentine Cranley and seconded by Mr John Salmon.

BRAY HARBOUR

In the mid-1700s ships docked at a small jetty close to Seapoint Road and less than 200m from Bray Bridge. This dock was only accessible for small craft; larger vessels would beach on the strand and transfer their cargo to smaller vessels. The larger vessels would have to wait for the next high tide to cast off. In 1863 a proposal was put forward to build a harbour at the southern end of the esplanade. The Bray Harbour Company could not raise sufficient capital for the project. The chief inhabitants of the town in 1866 applied to the government for Town Council status under the Towns Improvements (Ireland) Act 1854. The new Town Commissioners were to clash with the fishermen who dried their nets on the seafront.

The next proposal for a harbour or jetty came in 1867, when a 750m jetty was proposed jutting into the sea opposite Fitzwilliam Terrace. Objections came from the residents who feared that their property would be flooded and the project was shelved. The town council went ahead with its proposal to build a seawall over a kilometre long, and this was opened in 1885.

The next proposal for a harbour came in 1890, this was built around the river mouth and a small dock constructed by the railway company in 1854, when the railway bridge had been built across, blocking access to the jetty on Seapoint Road. The harbour, enclosing an area of eight acres, was completed in 1897, at a cost of £45,000. The harbour was last used commercially in 1943, and the harbour is used for pleasure craft today. In September 1957, Hurricane 'Carrie' caused storms that washed the lighthouse on the south pier into the sea.

AIR ACCIDENTS

There is only one licenced airfield in the area, at Powerscourt. This was the scene of an accident on 10 April 2010. The aircraft, a twin-seater Falco, was flown by its owner. The plane was returning from a thirty-minute flight over the Gorey area in Wexford. The plane landing gear struck a 30-foot tree close to the runway and the aircraft burst into flames. The passenger was killed instantly and the pilot died two days later in hospital. The Air Accident Unit found no technical faults with the aircraft. They noted that the pilot was experienced and had flown fifty-five different types of aircraft since he had first gained a licence in 1953.

A number of other air accidents have occurred in the Wicklow Mountains, mainly due to bad weather conditions. In 2008 a light aircraft crashed at Corriebrack Mountain. The pilot and three passengers were killed.

In 2004, a paraglider got into difficulties over Lough Bray, near Kippure Mountain, when he encountered very heavy turbulence.

The air accident that has gone down in folklore in the Enniskerry area is the flight carrying a group of French Girl Guides to an international Guide camp at Rathfarnham. The Irish Girl Guide movement had organised the camp and invited French and Dutch Guides to the event following the Second World War. The Junkers 52 aircraft left Le Bourget Airport in Paris with twenty-three French Girl Guides and seven crewmembers. The girls ranged in age from 14 to 22. Just after 2 p.m., Captain Habez lost radio contact with air traffic control in Dublin. The weather worsened as they approached the Irish Sea and there was very low cloud cover. Instead of taking the coastal route to Dublin Airport the plane drifted inland over the Wicklow Hills. The plane was flying at 1,800ft and just after 2 p.m. the under carriage of the plane struck the bogland on the slopes of Djouce Mountain and bounced 50 yards before coming to a halt. By some act of faith the plane did not catch fire and no one was killed.

The Garda set up an incident centre in Roundwood and fire brigades came from Bray and Dún Laoghaire. Local doctors from Bray and Enniskerry headed for Djouce Mountain along with local farmers who formed search parties. A fleet of ambulances and trained staff came from the Civil Defence, the Red Cross and St John's Ambulance service. The wreck of the plane was discovered by a search party about midnight and the injured were given first aid in a shooting hut belong to Lord Powerscourt. From the hut the injured were carried about four miles to the awaiting ambulances. The injured spent about two weeks in either St Michael's Hospital in Dún Loaghaire or St Bricin's Hospital in Dublin before being re-united with their families in France.

Fourteen of the survivors made a return trip to Ireland in 2011, they visited the crash site, the hospital and some of the rescue team.

MARITIME DISASTERS

Bray looks out on the Kish Bank, where over fifty ships have floundered since the mid-1700s. In the 1911 census of Enniskerry Patrick Woodcock lived at Kilamlin, Enniskerry and on 17 January 1905 he had married Elizabeth Collins, the daughter of Henry and Harriet Collins of Belfast. One of her brothers, John Collins, was a crew member on the RMS *Titanic*. On the night of 12 April 1912, when the ship hit an Iceberg and sank, John was saved and taken by the SS *Carpathia* to New York, where he landed on 18 April 1912. He returned to Belfast, where he died in 1941.

On the Second Class passenger list of the *Titanic*, the name J.J. Lamb appears. He paid £4 10s for his voyage to America from Cobh.

J.J. Lamb was a theatre manager and had travelled to France to engage some stage performers to come to America. He then went to Enniskerry to visit his elderly parents. After his visit to Enniskerry he headed to Cobh to catch the *Titanic* on her maiden voyage across the Atlantic. J.J. Lamb was returning to Philadelphia, where his sister Catherine lived. Sadly, James Lamb never made it to America, he perished in the cold waters of the North Atlantic.

The *Lusitania* has two links with Bray and with Cycle Polo. In 1915, a sailor, Albert A. Bestic, from County Dublin was in New York looking for a ship to take him back to the United Kingdom when he found employment as a third junior officer on the RMS *Lusitania*. One of the passengers on the *Lusitania* was Dr Ralph McCready, who had graduated from Trinity College and gone to gain medical experience at the Kellogs Battle Creek Sanitorium near Michigan. He took a ticket on the *Lusitania* from New York to Cobh, he was going to spend a short time at home before taking up a medical appointment in New Zealand. The ship was struck by a German torpedo off the Old Head of Kinsale, as it approached Cobh. Of the 1,962 passengers and crew, 1,191 lost their lives. Both Albert A. Bestic and Ralph McCready from Bray were saved and taken to Cobh.

Albert Bestic went on to man the SS *Isolda*, a ship employed by the Commissioners of Irish Lights to bring supplies to the lighthouses and lightships around the coast. On 19 December 1940, off the coast of Wexford, the *Isolda* was hit by a German bomb. Six of the crew were lost, but Captain Albert A. Bestic survived. He is sometimes referred to as Lucky/Unlucky Bestic, having been hit twice by German bombs in the First World War and the Second World War and survived both.

LOCOMOTIVES

There is one mode of transport that evokes memories of 'the age of steam', and this can only be the railways and steam trains. The big prize for the railway companies was the speed with which they could get the mail to London. There were two favoured routes from Dublin; the Dublin–Holyhead route via Birmingham to London, or the route down the east coast to Rosslare and then on to Fishguard and finally to London. How quickly the shipping companies could cross the Irish Sea was the key to success. The main person driving the development of the railway in Ireland was William Dargan. For a short while he lived in the town and was also a Bray Town Commissioner. He took a great interest in developing the Esplanade in Bray, along with tourism, and Bray acquired the name 'the Irish Brighton'. This was helped, by the fact that Bray was serviced by two routes from the capital city, Dublin. There was an inland line from Harcourt Street via Foxrock, and the coastal route from Westland Row via Kingstown (Dún Laoghaire), where passengers would transfer onto the Atmospheric Railway as far as Dalkey and head south by steam power. The railway companies changed their names as they advanced southwards. The Dublin and Kingstown Railway was established in 1831, and they opened the railway line between Westland Row and Kingstown in 1834, with a journey time of fourteen minutes. Within three years, a committee was formed to report on the advantages of running the railway to Bray.

The obstacles en route were threefold: land ownership, the need for tunnels at Killiney, and the wide river crossing at Bray. An act of parliament was sought in 1846 to establish a railway line to Bray via Foxrock, Dundrum, Milltown and Harcourt Street in Dublin. This line was to serve the community of South Dublin and North Wicklow from 1854 up to 1959, when CIÉ decided to close it in a cost-cutting exercise. The cutting of the first sod of the railway around the formidable Bray Head took place at the height of the famine in 1847, and employed 500 men in the mammoth task of tunnelling three tunnels and laying tracks close to the cliff edge in a time when the main tools were pick, shovel, block and tackle for lifting heavy weights. The line between Bray and Greystones was opened in 1855. The line between was closed a number of times due to rockfall, the most notable been in March 1857, and again in 1876, 1888 and 1917. The railway station for Bray was to be on the north side of the river-mouth. The railway company came up with the solution of narrowing the river upstream, and they were able to narrow the river crossing. This then posed a second problem: by building a bridge they would cut off access to the Bray shipping dock close to the town.

Although plans had been drawn up for a harbour at the southern end of the esplanade, this had yet to get parliamentary approval. So the railway company decided to build a small dock on the seaward side of the new railway bridge. So the building of the Bray Railway Station was begun in 1853. The railway company was very class conscious, and on the Dublin, Kingstown and Bray Railway line there were a number of different carriages available: first, second, closed second and third class, which meant that the railway station had to have three entrances and exits. The first-class passengers had their own booking office and a ladies' and gentlemen's waiting room with an open fire. The second-class passengers entered the station from the railway yard beside the newsagents, which is now a coffee dock. The third class would enter the station from Albert Avenue, and after going up a flight of stairs the passengers would be on the station platform near the old gasworks and the turn-table. The official opening of Bray Railway Station took place on 8 July 1854 with pomp and ceremony, and the first trains carrying passengers departed Bray at 6.30 a.m. on 10 July 1854 without any fuss or fanfare.

At the height of the railway in Bray, over 200 men and women were employed by the station, including the platform staff, porters, the booking-office staff, administration staff, engineering staff, telegraph lines men, staff in the railway sheds, the staff in the goods yard, and those employed in making deliveries in the town. Mr Joseph Kennedy was appointed the first stationmaster at Bray with a salary of £80 per annum, he was also given a fine residence in the station yard or an allowance in lieu, the house was sold at a public auction in 1982.

More name changes were announced in 1906, when the Dublin, Wicklow and Wexford Railway Company became the Dublin and South Eastern Railway Company on 1 January 1907. The Railway Company was a major landowner in Bray and in 1919 they gave the site for a War Memorial in Bray, a Celtic cross with three bronze plaques bearing the names of 155 people from Bray who were lost in the First World War. The railway company encouraged tourists to come to Bray, this was done in various ways, they built a platform beside Bray Cove baths and another platform at Woodbrook Golf Club, they carried military and civilian bands free of charge, they provided bathing boxes on the esplanade for ladies, they sponsored regattas in the town, and cheap day trips. This in turn gave a good return to the shareholders of the company.

In April 1927 the company built a second platform in Bray alongside the 1894 signal box, on the seaward side of the station. Today, when passengers alight from the trains at this platform they are greeted by a series of mural mosaics depicting the development of the railway.

During the late 1930s and early 1940s, a new style of traction engine was developed by Dr James Drumm, to which he gave his name, the Drumm Battery Train. The locomotives had a series of heavy-duty batteries strapped to the under-carriage of the train. The batteries on the trains were recharged overnight in Dublin and at Bray. In the 1940s it was decided that diesel was the preferred option for powering the locomotives. With another name change on the way following the 1944 Transport Act, the Dublin & South Eastern Railway Company was taken over by CIÉ.

In 1952 the roof of Bray Railway Station caught fire and it was the first call out for the new fire-tender acquired by the Bray Urban District Council.

In 1956 new locomotives were introduced, and in 1961 the colour of the livery on the rolling stock changed from green to orange and black and, with a few exceptions on main line services, where first class remains, CIÉ introduced a single standard passenger class, and Bray Railway Station was remodelled.

In 1966, Bray station was renamed Daly Station in honour of Edward Daly, who took part in the Easter Rising. When Bray people heard the announcement, the first remark was 'Who is Edward Daly and what is his connection with Bray?' A memorial plaque was erected near the station-master's office.

In 1979, CIÉ announced that it was going to upgrade the railway between Howth and Bray and the new service would be called the 'DART', Dublin Area Rapid Transit, a railway system for the twenty-first century with new electric trains which would provide a smoother, faster service and would be in place by mid-1984, at a cost of £66 million. The new carriages would have push-button doors and seating for 144 people, and the trains would be built in Germany. In February 1983, the first of the new carriages arrived at Dublin Port. In July 1984, the new service was up and running and the colour of the livery changed back to green.

With the introduction of the new electric trains, a whole symphony of sounds disappeared at Bray Railway Station. The old wooden gates at the level crossing were replaced with a set of electric gates. The banging of the doors of the train by the guard as he made sure everyone was safely on the train also disappeared. All these sounds disappeared overnight, to be replaced by a countdown clock showing the departure time of the next train. There was no need for the turn-table or the water tower, although it still stands idle on the platform. The snapping of the wires pulling the arms of the signals into place also stopped. The poles carrying the telegraphic information from the signal cabin were no longer required. Nor the ticket checker shouting, 'have your tickets ready for inspection', or the clip of the punch as it made contact with the cardboard ticket. Today, there are automated barriers to gain access to the platforms. The tannoy announcement for each train is now seldom used.

RAILWAY ACCIDENTS IN IRELAND

The *East Oregonian* newspaper in the United States on 16 September 1910, carried an article with the title, 'The Earl of Meath has a Joke'.

[Lord Meath] founder of the Hospital Saturday Fund, where the poor can save a small amount each week towards an illness. The Lord is also President of the Church Army and is engaged in other philanthropic organisations. An American was a guest of Lord Meath at his home in Killruddery in Ireland. The American was very eloquently expounding the merits of the American Railroads to the disadvantage of the Irish lines.

'Well' said the Earl of Meath, hiding a smile, 'I know there is a least one railway in Ireland where collisions are absolutely impossible.' 'Indeed,' said the American eagerly, 'How is it done? What's the system?'

'Oh you see,' replied the earl, 'the company has only one locomotive'.

9

SPORT AND ENTERTAINMENT

ARCADIA BALLROOM THE BALLROOM OF ROMANCE

The Arcadia Ballroom, part of the International Hotel complex, came into its own after the end of the First World War. The then owner engaged Edward Harrison's band to entertain the holiday-makers and courting couples from Dublin. Edward and his band played at the Arcadia for two decades. On 1 June 1947, the new owner of the Arcadia, Patrick Corscadden announced a new resident band. Bill Carter and his band entertained to capacity audiences. The Arcadia ballroom was located on a quarter of an acre, with a floor space of 16,700 sq. ft and a mezzanine level of 5,800 sq. ft, and could cater for 5,000 patrons as one of the largest dance halls in Ireland. On special occasions, dancing was from 9 p.m. to 3 a.m. Córas Iompair Éireann ran 'Dance Excursions' in the 1950s, combining a train and dance ticket. The Arcadia attracted the stars of the music world, including Tom Jones, Roy Orbinson, Joe Dolan and the Drifters, Joe Loss and the Melody Aces, The Miami (the Irish version of the Beatles), and Phil Murtagh and his dance band, Eurovision singer Sandie Shaw preformed in the Arcadia in 1968.

In July 1965, another Eurovision singer, Butch Moore, narrowly escaped injury when he began to sing 'Walking the streets in the Rain'. He was pulled off the stage with the surge of the crowd moving forward. In 1964, the Bachelors preformed their first home-coming gig after a successful tour of Britain and USA, their performance was in the new Arcadia Ballroom. After the dances upwards of twenty-five double-decker buses were on hand to take patrons home to Dublin, Kilcoole and Delgany.

The old ballroom was destroyed by fire on 24 October 1962. The new ballroom attracted rock and pop groups and was known as Film-More – West. The hall was rented out to youth and community groups for a number of years in the early 1970s, including an annual Bray Youth Expo hosted by Bray Youth Council and the Flower and Vegetables Shows held by Bray and District Horticultural Society. In 1971, the Arcadia Ballroom was put up for public auction, and in the mid-1970s the ballroom was converted to a Cash and Carry Warehouse, leaving only faded memories of Bray's music industry.

ST MARY'S GAA CLUB, ENNISKERRY

St Mary's GAA club was founded in Enniskerry following a meeting in the school house in 1956. The club was developed by Joe Walsh, Sean Woodcock, Christopher White and Tom Corcoran, the schoolmaster. A club existed in the village as far back as 1889, but the newly formed St Mary's was to earn county awards in 1962, when the team, consisting of Sean Murphy, Jack Kearns, Liam Keogh, Des Burton, Mick MacDonald, Christy McDonald, Declan Burton, Paddy Kelly, Sean Woodcock, Christy Byrne, Noel Keogh, Vincent Butler, Gerry Fitzmorris, Joe Delahaunt and Jimmy Byrne, lifted the County Wicklow Junior Football Championship Cup. The club went on to become League winners in 1970, they won the Schwepps Cup in 1971, and became Intermediate League winners in 1972. In 1978, the writer Frederick Forsythe, decided to donate a field to St Mary's Club at Parknasillogue, the club developed a clubhouse and laid out the pitches. The president-Elect of the GAA, Paddy Buggy opened the complex on 5 July 1981. The club enjoys good support from the local community.

BRAY EMMETS

The club was founded in 1885, and their first game was played in November 1885 against the County Dublin Club, based in Dalkey. The first County Football Championship took place in 1887, and the Bray team played Rathnew, Wicklow Town and Avondale. The most remarkable piece of history took place in 1902, when Bray Emmets played for Dublin and won the All-Ireland Championship. The win is recorded as a Dublin All-Ireland win. But Wicklow claims it as the only time Wicklow won an All-Ireland final. The club originally played its games in the Vevay, the People's Park and Novara Avenue Sports Grounds. The latter sports ground is now the site of apartments and the Mermaid Theatre. Fr Brady came to Bray in 1914 and secured the Novara Avenue Sports Ground as the permanent home of Bray Emmets.

In the 1950s a second GAA team emerged in Bray called St Kevin's, and both team coexisted until the 1980s when they merged to become an enlarged Bray Emmets. Plans were drawn up for a new town centre, taking over the former home of the parish priest of Bray Parishes, St Cronan's on the Main Street, and the adjoining property of Novara Avenue Sportsground. This would create new Town Council Offices, a theatre, a health centre and housing. Bray Emmets moved to a plot of ground on Old Connaught Avenue. The first pitch was opened in 2000, 130 years after the founding of the club.

BRAY BOXING

Katie Taylor and Adam Nolan placed Bray Boxing Club on the world map when they were selected to represent Ireland at the Olympic Games in 2012. Katie had already gained international recognition with national, European and world titles. Bray Boxing Club can be traced back to March 1929, when *The Irish Times* newspaper carried a photograph of the members of the Dublin University boxing team, which was going to take on members of the Bray Boxing Club in the Arcadia ballroom.

Boxing in Bray had humble beginnings, with competitions against military teams at boxing tournaments during the Second World War and during Bray Civic Festivals. After the war, a boxing club was revived in the town, with Fr Brady and Yann Renard-Goulet establishing St Bridget's Youth Club, which taught boxing. The youth club used a hall at Brighton Terrace. A boxing club was founded and rented rooms in Fatima Hall near the railway station. The club later moved to a building known as An Lar on the Lower Dargle, and in the mid-1970s they were renting rooms in the Little Flower Hall off Main Street. With no permanent home and having to pack away equipment after each session, the club was finding it hard to survive. But, with dedicated people who promoted boxing as a skill, such as Al Morris, Tommy Traynor, Tony Pouch, Mark and Tony O'Reilly, the club was saved and saw the birth of St Fergal's Boxing Club in 1995, with Peter Taylor and Tony Kelly at the helm. The club was using the Ballyaltrim community centre, and it became known as Ballyaltrim Boxing Club.

In 2007, a new headquarters for boxing in Bray was established when the organisers of the Boxing Club persuaded the Town Council to give them the use of a disused shed at the harbour. The shed is one of the items in Harry Kernoff's painting of Bray Harbour in 1941. The shed came to public attention in 2012 when the media outlined the conditions that our Olympic Champions were training in. Compared to that of other nations, the training facility in Bray lacked basic equipment. In response, the government and the Town Council announced an upgrade of the building at a cost of €300,000, and it was opened in 2014.

TELEVISION AND RADIO

Kippure (Cipiur) Mountain played a vital role in early television in Ireland, as it was a pivotal part of the jigsaw of relay signals across the whole of Ireland. It is hard to believe that in 1960 a television signal on 425 and 625 frequency was only picked up in 100,000 homes in Ireland. The story started when Lord Powerscourt sold two parcels of land to the Broadcasting Authority. The first site was for the control room, accommodation, garage that stored the off-road vehicles and a snowplough, and for the 127m mast. The second parcel of land, also sold in 1959, allowed access from the Sally Gap Road to the control centre at the top of Kippure Mountain. During the summer of 1961 anyone with a television in Bray and Enniskerry could tune into the test card of the new Radió Telifís Éireann, and the voice of Count John McCormack. On New Year's Eve, outside the Gresham Hotel in O'Connell Street, the service went live.

RTÉ programmes started at 5 p.m. in the evening and the station closed down at 11.15 p.m., with an Aer Lingus plane taking off and the screen fading to black. There was no television service on Good Friday, just the test card and music. PYE Television were selling new single-channel televisions for 70 guineas, and extras included a remote control for 3 guineas and the legs that could be attached to the base of the television were 1½ guineas. You also could get a hire purchase deal at £8 10s a week with a free indoor aerial. The cost of a television licence was £4.

A blizzard on 12 February 1963 resulted in ice forming on the television mast and caused a break in transmission on RTÉ for 43 minutes that evening.

GOLF AND WAR WOUNDED

Bray Golf Club decided that all entrance fees for Easter Monday 1915 would be given to the Princess Patricia Hospital for Wounded Soldiers in Bray. Mrs Glenn and the Bray War Work Party had made 1,629 dressing for use in the hospital over the past year, and an additional 1,200 dressings which were sent to France and Mesopotamia.

HOLE IN ONE AT WOODBROOK

On 7 April 1945, Bernard Lynch of Woodbrook got a hole-in-one. What made this remarkable is that another Bernard Lynch who was not related also got a hole-in-one. The odds of this happening are about three million to one.

10

YOUTH

GIRLS' FRIENDLY SOCIETY

The first meeting of the Central Council of the Girls' Friendly Society (Irish Branch) was held on 22 February 1877, in the Royal Marine Hotel, Bray. The attendance was small, four ladies and two gentlemen: Viscountess Powerscourt, Viscountess Monck, Mrs Green, Mrs La Touche, Revd Scott and Revd Cross. The meeting decided to form an Irish Branch, independent of the Central Council in London. The meeting was adjourned until October 1877, when the Countess of Meath was elected President of the Irish Central Council.

SCOUTING

Since 1908, Scouts have camped on the land at Kilruddery, the home of the Earl of Meath, and Powerscourt Estate, the home of Lord Powerscourt, the first District Commissioner for the County Wicklow Boy Scout Association. In the 1920s, at the World Jamboree held in England, the Irish delegation was led by Lord Powerscourt, the Earl of Meath and Sir Stanley Cochrane, the director of Cantrell and Cochrane, who lived at Woodbrook near Bray.

AN ÓIGE

County Wicklow is the jewel in the crown of the Irish Youth Hostel Association, An Óige. The association was formed in May 1931, and it was soon recognised that walking in County Wicklow would form an important part of the Association, which had its headquarters located at 39 Mountjoy Square. The first hostel was opened in 1931 at Lough

Dan near Roundwood, in the heart of Wicklow. The growth of the hostel movement in County Wicklow can be linked with walking routes published in the *Evening Herald* newspaper. The first article written by the renowned walker J.B. Malone appeared in the newspaper in 1938, the same year that Knockree Hostel near Enniskerry was opened in an eighteenth-century farmhouse on the Powerscourt Estate.

A circular walking route, starting and ending in Enniskerry, and taking in Walker's Rock, Curtlestown and Kilmalin, was published in the *Evening Herald* on 28 April 1939. In total J.B. Malone published 959 walking routes over thirty-seven years in the newspapers. In 1982, the first stage of the Wicklow Way was opened in Marley Park. The Wicklow Way stretches from Marley Park in the foothills of the Dublin and Wicklow Mountains, to Clonegal at the foothills of the Blackstairs Mountains. A vast part of the walk passes over the lands once owned by Lord Powerscourt.

CHILDREN'S LIBRARY

Charles Stewart Parnell died in 1891, and there was a proposal to have a national memorial at Avondale, the former home of Parnell. The residents of Bray wanted a county memorial. After some discussion, the County Memorial Committee planned to build a lighthouse of mirrors on Sugarloaf Mountain, with the rays from the mirrors shining on the counties Kildare, Dublin, Meath and Wicklow. A fund of over £150 was collected but fell far short of the amount needed to build a lighthouse of mirrors so the £150 lay dormant in an account. The librarian in Bray Library planned to build a children's section in 1953, and the Library Committee need to raise funds. Someone on the committee remembered the dormant Parnell Memorial Fund. The committee approached the last trustee of the Parnell Fund, who agreed to give the money to the children's section of the library. The committee proposed that a bronze bust of Charles Stewart Parnell would be cast to remind the children were the funds had come from to build the extension to the library. A special section in the library was dedicated to books on Irish history, with special reference to Charles Stewart Parnell.

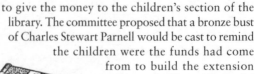

11

LAW AND MAYHEM

A SHOOTING IN THE WOODS

In early September 1780, a melancholy affair took place near Enniskerry. A young man named Hanson, who was a volunteer in Lord Powerscourt's army, happened to be with Lord Powerscourt's park keeper and another man, at his house, when a shot went off some distance away. They guessed that someone had killed a deer, so Hanson took up his gun and went towards where the shot came from, with the other men following him. He soon came upon two brothers named Cooley, one of whom had a buck on his back. Hanson yelled that they must stop or he would shoot them, which they instantly did. But the fellow who had the buck threw it down, took the gun off his brother and fired at Mr Hanson, who dropped, having received the ball in his breast. He died a short time after the keeper came up.

The villains escaped while the park keeper's attention was taken up in giving Mr Hanson his assistance, but over 200 volunteers went in pursuit of them. In February 1781, Joseph Cooley was arrested in Arklow by a force of 200 of Lord Powerscourt volunteers and he was brought to justice.

STORM OF 1839

On 6/7 January 1839 a violent storm swept over Ireland. In Bray, Mr Putland's home suffered material damage and many trees were felled by the wind. The rainfall on the roads at Bray, Loughlinstown, Killruddery and Powerscourt made them impassable until a late hour on 7 January 1839. On the evening of 6 January, a woman living in a cottage opposite Mr Putland's lodge was killed by a falling chimney; her sister, who was sleeping with her, escaped with some bruises.

DEVELOPMENT OF BRAY AND NORTH WICKLOW

A number of pieces of legislation changed the fortunes of Bray and North Wicklow. The first was the formation of the Dublin & Wicklow and Wexford Railway Company in 1846, with the opening of Bray Railway Station in 1854. The Town Improvements (Ireland) Act 1854 saw the chief inhabitants of the town incorporate themselves into a governing body on 9 October 1857. On 23 July 1866, Bray received Township status.

MR SWIFTE VISITED ENNISKERRY EIGHT TIMES IN 1890

In 1890, a Dublin man named Mr Swifte was accused of embezzling £180 from his employer, Mr P.A. Chance, a Dublin solicitor of Westmoreland Street. When questioned by the police how he spent the money, the man claimed that on eight Sundays he took a number of his lady friends to Enniskerry and to the Bray Regatta. Each Sunday he had allowed £2 10s for the carriage (brake), £1 10s for dinner, and £1 for refreshments. Asked if he could remember the ladies he took to Enniskerry, he replied the he took Miss Hodges twice, with Miss Fagan three times, and on three different occasions he took two ladies, Miss Breslin and Miss Cleary. He also gave Miss Cleary a watch. He made other trips to the Strawberry Beds and to Howth. In all, he only spent £74 17s 6d.

SHOOTING RABBITS 1909

In the House of Commons in September 1909, Mr Field MP, asked the Solicitor-General of Ireland whether he was aware that in a recent case in Wicklow County, near Bray, two members of the constabulary in plain clothes had demanded to see a licence from a man who was carrying a gun; whether, on his refusal to do so unless they showed him their legal authority, he was brought to barracks and subsequently fined, notwithstanding that he had produced his licence; whether this was the usual procedure; and whether he would arrange that when members of the constabulary asked for a licence to be shown they would disclose their authority to do so?

Mr Redmond Barry replied on behalf of the Solicitor-General of Ireland to Mr Field's question, stating that, on the occasion in question, an acting-sergeant and constable of the Royal Irish Constabulary, who had been specially sent out to detect breaches of the Gun Licence Act, met a stranger carrying a gun who refused either to produce his licence or to give his name and address, as required by the act, though informed by the police of their rank. He was arrested and brought to the barracks, and was subsequently brought before a special Petty Sessions Court, charged with the offence of refusing to give his name and address while carrying a gun for which he refused to produce a licence, and was fined £10, mitigated, as provided by the act, to £2 10s, which he paid.

In July 1909, at Bray Police Barracks the man, who was carrying a single-barrel breach-loading gun, gave his name as John Riston of Dublin. The purpose of his outing to County Wicklow was to shoot rabbits.

CHILDREN NOT GOING TO SCHOOL, 1911

The Hansard debates of the House of Commons are the most unlikely place to discover a piece of local history and social conditions in Enniskerry in 1911. However, the House of Commons records for 7 March 1911 show that Mr John Muldoon, MP for East Wicklow, asked the Chief Secretary of Ireland and cabinet minister Mr Birrel, whether his attention had been drawn to the language used by Captain the Hon. De Vere Pery, RM, at the last Enniskerry Petty Sessions, when he lectured a poor widow, in receipt of 6s a week for herself and six children, for not sending her children to school; and whether he intended to take any steps in the matter?

Mr Birrell, Chief Secretary of Ireland, replied on behalf of the government. 'My attention has been called to the matter referred to. I understand that the School Attendance Committee investigated the case, and gave this woman every opportunity of explaining her reason for keeping her children from school. This she neglected to do, and there was no other course open to the committee but to apply to the magistrates for an attendance order. On her refusal to obey the order made by the magistrates she was again summoned by the committee, leaving the magistrates no other course but to convict. The widow is in receipt of 6s a week outdoor relief. She resides in a labourer's cottage, the rent of which is paid for her. Two brothers reside in the house with her, one of whom earns at least 17s a week. She earns a little herself, and has a son also in employment getting fair wages. Captain Pery's language on the occasion calls for no action on the part of the Government.'

Thomas Philip Le Fanu, who was born at Summerhill, Enniskerry was private secretary to the Chief Secretary of Ireland, the Rt Hon. Augustine Birrell for the period 1910–1913.

The widow at the centre of the crisis was Mrs Catherine Mooney, who had three school-going children aged 13, 11 and 9. She was summoned to court by the school attendance officer, Mr Patrick Clarke. In the court she claimed that she had not sufficient clothing or boots for her children, and it would be dangerous to their health if they attended school. The magistrate stated that the children should walk barefoot to school, and he imposed fines and court costs that in total came to 15 shillings.

Following the court case some unnamed benefactor paid the court costs and fines. Mrs Mooney received charitable donations that allowed her to purchase clothing and boots for all her children.

MRS MARTIN'S MAINTENANCE PAYMENTS FROM A CRIPPLED SOLDIER

Mrs Annie Martin appeared before the Dublin Southern Police Court, and she claimed that he husband, Mr Ernest Martin, was six months behind in maintenance payments at the rate of £2 per week. In her deposition she stated that before she married Mr Martin she was married to Mr Spickman. She was employed as an actress in Mr George Edwards' Company. Mr Spickman left her property valued £1,000 and £7 per week provided she did not marry again. She used the £1,000 to establish Mr Martin in a quantity surveyor business in Nottinghamshire and subsequently in Dublin. Mr Martin established the business in Molesworth's Street in Dublin and they lived on Marlbourgh Road in Donnybrook. Mr Martin deserted her in 1905 and went to Australia. When war broke out in Europe, Mr Martin joined the Australian Army and was posted to France. He was wounded and sent to a hospital in Manchester. Because he was born in Ireland he was sent to the Princess Patricia Hospital in Bray. Mr Magee, a Bray solicitor, represented Mr Martin. It was stated that Mr Martin was a corporal in the army and had an unblemished record. He was not in a position to pay the £46 in maintance payments, but hoped to raise the money within a week. Mr Magee looked for an adjournment of the case for a week. When the case came up the following week, Mr Magee stated that his client had made payment to Mrs Martin.

FORCED LABOUR ROAD TRENCHING, 1921

A party of Irish Volunteers, said to number over a hundred, visited every house in the village of Shankill, County Dublin on the evening of 29 March 1921 and all available able-bodied young men were marched to a place now known as the Vale, where they were supplied with shovels and picks. They were marched to the hilly district of Enniskerry known as Ballyman, and were ordered to dig trenches across the road. After this was done they were forced to dig a second trench across the Bray and Enniskerry Road. Two members of the Dublin Mounted Police came upon the men trenching by accident. The men were searched by the police and temporarily detained in a house used by the gardener of Sir Timothy O'Brien. On 30 March 1921 a military detachment was dispatched to the area and they compelled the villagers in Enniskerry and the residents of Ballyman to fill in the trenches.

BRAY & MUSIC, 1926

On 11 August 1926, the St James Brass and Reed Band gave a performance on the grand bandstand on Bray seafront. To the south of bandstand there was an enclosed area where patrons could purchase a programme and a deckchair to sit on. The programmes were sold for 6 pence and the deckchair rental was 1 shilling. The band played a tune, 'Lilac Thyme', and the Performance Rights Association sought royalties under the Copyright Act of 1911. When the case came before the courts, the legal team for the Bray Town Commissioners pointed out that the act referred to performances in England and made no reference to Ireland. So when the action was filed against the Bray Town Commissioners and the Bray Urban District Council, they claimed the Copyright Act of 1911 had no jurisdiction in Ireland. The Privy Council upheld the Bray Urban District Council reading of the 1911 Act and rejected the claim by the Performance Rights Association for their action for royalties of £228. Within weeks of the Privy Council produced a new Copyright Act, which was passed by Dáil Éireann.

TURF AND TREES, 1941

In January 1942, Lord Powerscourt and Mr John Jordan appeared before Bray District Court, charged with not having permission from the Department of Lands to fell trees in the Glencree valley. Lord Powerscourt and Mr Jordan were required to give twenty-one days' statutory notice to the department.

Lord Powerscourt defended himself; he said in the spring of 1941 there was a fuel famine. He cast about his mind to find a way to help the poor. He gave 700 acres of bog land to Wicklow County Council free of charge and about 200 acres to a committee in Bray free of charge, for the production of turf. In July 1941, it was reported that a person named Jordan with a gang of men, was also working on a bog in Glencree without his permission. He went up there, prepared to turn him off. He found Mr Jordan, and approached him in no good temper. In the course of the conservation he explained why he was there and that he had got permission from someone who had no right to give it. He further explained what desperate straits many poor people in the locality of Crumlin, near Dublin City, were in. How they had nothing to burn and could not cook their food. He had about thirty unemployed boys from Crumlin cutting turf, who knew nothing about it. Mr Jordan said if he had done wrong he would take all his men away at once.

Lord Powerscourt said:

I was very much impressed by the truth of Mr Jordan. He told me all about the suffering that was going on. He was responsible for fuelling the homes of 4,000 poor people's homes. I thought, why should I confine my help to the people of County Wicklow. In August, Mr Jordan rang me and said he had cut out 2,000 tons of turf, but he greatly feared the he would not be able to save half of it and with the onset of winter, he asked me to give him some timber. I at first refused, but was impressed by the conditions in Crumlin. I had heard from two different sources that Mr Jordan was telling the truth. His sources told him that people in Crumlin were tearing up the floors of their houses to cook with. So I told Mr Jordan that I had two small woods in the Glencree valley that I would give him for nothing, but he would have to harvest the timber. Mr Jordan came down to the Glencree Valley and we went over the woods. Mr Jordan agreed to buy the timber at the price of one shilling per ton. My only condition was that the fuel would only go to the poor in Crumlin as timber was on sale in Dublin at eight shillings per ton.

Both woods were purchased by him on 1 September 1941. I then applied to the Forestry Branch on behalf of Mr Jordan as the woods had previously been my property. I applied for the first wood on 30 August and the second wood on 4 September. Nothing happened for a fortnight and on 11 September, Mr Jordan began felling the trees. On 12 September I received two prohibition notices from the Forestry Department. I appealed at once but did not get an answer. This was the first prohibition order I ever received. Then I was summoned by the Department to appear in court for cutting 35 trees in one place and 64 trees in the other.

District Justice O'Sullivan in Bray District Court heard from the State solicitors Mr A.B. Cullen and Mr Anderson, and Mr Swords from the Department of Lands, who said that felling had taken place prior to the twenty-one days' notice required and the felling had taken place without permission. Mr W.J. Norman, solicitor, represented Mr Jordan. Justice O'Sullivan then applied the Probation Act to Lord Powerscourt and Mr Jordan.

SCOUTS DISCOVER ESCAPED PRISONER, 1952

Ever since the beginning of Scouting in 1908, scouts have been given the freedom to roam the estates of Lord Powerscourt and the Earl of Meath. Both Lord Powerscourt and the Earl of Meath were friends of the founder of scouting, Lord Robert Baden Powell.

On 7 March 1952 a man named James Borthwick escaped from Mountjoy Prison while painting the Governor's house. On 25 March 1952, a group of Dublin Scouts were camping in Powerscourt, in an area known as White's Field Wood. While out foraging for wild foods in a clearing they came across ashes from a fire and a dixie full of water. They began to investigate and saw a pair of socks hanging on bushes nearby. They suddenly heard snoring come from the bushes nearby. At first they thought it might be a tramp. They recalled the words of the Scout Warden Percy Scott to be on the lookout for an escaped prisoner who was still at large. They returned to Mr Scott, the Scout Warden, at his cottage on the estate. The scouts had their suspicion that the person in the shelter made of branches might be the escaped prisoner. Mr Scott informed Guard Flanagan in Enniskerry, who came at once. The scouts and Guard Flanagan proceed to the manmade shelter, inside which they found Mr James Borthwick, who had been at large for eighteen days. In the shelter there was a quantity of tinned food, a mirror, shaving equipment and cooking utensils. Mr Borthwick had 8 pence in cash in his possession. Mr Borthwick was returned to Mountjoy Prison and was further charged with thirteen counts of house-breaking and larceny of goods valued £31 13s 7d from scouts huts on Powerscourt Estate. The goods included camping equipment, blankets and tinned food. He was also charged with stealing a sheep the property of Mr Norman C. Walker of Enniskerry.

12

WILDLIFE

Some of the place names in the district give us a hint of the birds that can be found there: Ravenswell, Eagles Nest, Quill Lane, Grouse Hill, Swan Brook. You do not need to be an expert to discover the flora and fauna of North Wicklow – Just a keen eye and a field guide of plants and animals will give many hours of enjoyment. The flora and fauna of Bray and Enniskerry have been recorded over the years and this first-hand information is very useful.

The geology was recorded by **Thomas Oldham** (1816-1878). In the Cambrian rocks of Bray Head he discovered fossils. At the time of this discovery in 1840 these were the oldest fossils known anywhere in the world. His fellow naturalist, Edward Forbes (1815-1854) suggested that the fossils should be named 'Oldhamia' in honour of their discoverer.

Anne L. Massy (1867-1931) grew up in Enniskerry, and by the age of twenty was a keen ornithologist and was one of the founders of the Irish Society for the Protection of Birds, in 1904. She discovered Redstarts (Ruticilla phoenicurus) breeding on the Powerscourt Estate in 1887. It remains an extreme rarity. She went on to become a world expert in the classification of molluscs. She was vital in the passing of the first legislation for nature conservation in Ireland, the Wild Birds Protection Act of 1930.

When we think of wildlife in Ireland we think of one name, **Eamon De Buitlear** (1930 -2013). His interest in wildlife began as a child living by the Dargle River in Bray. Since then his hobby became his job. His television programme, Amuigh Faoin Spéir, with the artist Gerrit van Gelderen, introduced a generation to the wildlife of Ireland. Many of the images came from Wicklow, including the sea birds on the cliff at Bray Head, the kingfishers on the Dargle River, and birds of prey on the Powerscourt Estate. The paths and trails over Bray Head were named De Buitlear Way by Wicklow County Council in 2014 in honour of Eamon.

Richard M. Barrington (1849-1915) lived at Fassaroe near Bray and spent his life recording rainfall and crop yields. He is best known for his scientific paper on the migration of birds observed from the lighthouses of Ireland and he predicted the 1905 flood of the Dargle River in 1898. His bird collection is housed in the Natural History Museum of Ireland and the Ulster Museum.

Reginald Ernest Cusack (1893-1915) was educated at Aravon, Bray. He developed a keen interest in insects and moths, collecting many specimens on the slopes of Bray Head. He was killed in France in the First World War, and his collection of butterflies, moths and insects were donated to the Natural History Museum of Ireland.

Oscar Merne (1943-2013) was the first warden of the Wexford Wildfowl Reserve. He was one of the founders of Bird Watch Ireland. With his work in the Parks and Wildlife Service, he identified over 100 areas of special protection under the EU Birds Directive 1979, including Bray Head. Oscar lived in Bray and each year monitored the migrant birds and was involved in the ringing program to trace the movements of birds.

Dr Tom Curtis is a native of Bray who still lives in the town. He is a botanist and one of the authors of the *Irish Red Data Book of Vasculat Plants* (1988). Tom has recorded the plants that grow in County Wicklow.

Sir Arthur Purves Phayre is buried in the graveyard at Enniskerry. He was appointed first British commissioner of Burma and then Governor of Mauritius. While there he had a bird, tortoise, squirrel and a monkey called after him. He retired to Bray and died on 14 December 1885. He was buried in St Patrick's graveyard, Enniskerry.

COASTAL CLIFFS

The coastal cliffs at Bray Head attracting a wide range of seabirds, including gulls, fulmars, cormorants, shags, razorbills, guillemots and puffins. The summer birds like swallows, swifts, house martins, chiffchaffs, and other members of the warbler family, can be seen close up during the months of April and May. Higher up on Bray Head the screech skylark can be heard. A keen observer may see sparrowhawks, kestrels, buzzards and other birds of prey in the area.

Kingfishers and dippers can be seen on the Dargle River, while pheasants, wood pigeons, magpies and rooks get along with the sheep on the hills.

FISHING RECORDS

The Guinness Book of Records for 1972 has two Irish Angling Records for Bray. The first is the greater spotted dogfish of 19lb 12oz caught by Michael Courage at Bray on 6 July 1969. The second record is for a sea trout of 12lb 0oz caught by T. Regan on the River Dargle at Bray on 3 October 1958.

ROYAL FOREST OF GLENCREE

In 1229 King Henry III granted permission to Luke, Archbishop of Dublin, to carry out the deforesting of certain lands formerly belonging to the see of Glendalough. It is certain that a royal forest was formed in Glencree in County Wicklow. In 1244 sixty does and twenty bucks were ordered to be taken alive from the King's Park nearest to the port of Chester and be sent to Dalkey and delivered to the King's Treasurer in Dublin to stock the King's Park at Glencry (Glencree).

When it comes to the tallest tree in Ireland, it is a Douglas Fir standing 61.6m (202ft) on the river walk in Powerscourt estate. This makes it the seventh tallest tree in Europe.

There are a number of State forests in the Dargle Valley:

Location	Date of first acquisition	Area (acres)	Planted
Ballinagee	21/05/1942	4,050	3,270
Enniskerry	16/12/1929	1,617	1,500
Glencree	03/02/1923	1,983	1,902

SIKA DEER

Another import of deer took place in 1861, when Lord Powerscourt introduced Japanese Sika to his Deer Park near the Powerscourt Waterfall. It was not long before the Sika deer escaped and mixed with the native red deer.

The Irish Naturalist's Journal of 1934 estimated that there were 500–600 Sika deer on Lord Powerscourt's estate.

THE EAGLE AND THE TERRIER

The Penny Magazine, published on 25 April 1835, carried a story about an eagle in the Wicklow Mountains on Lord Powerscourt's estate, near Lough Tay. In March 1769, some gentlemen were hunting near Lough Tay when a large eagle hastily descended and seized their terrier. The wings of the eagle measured 7ft across. The eagle soared a couple of feet before dropping the terrier.

BLACK GROUSE, 1868

An attempt to introduce black grouse to County Wicklow was made by Lord Powerscourt in 1868. Lord Powerscourt obtained permission from the Duke of Roxburgh to send over his head gamekeeper, Mr James Anton, to Floors Castle near Kelso in the Scottish Borders. Mr Anton returned to Enniskerry with twenty-five black grouse eggs. Four birds were released into the wild at Powerscourt deer park, but none survived.

Mr Anton was no stranger to Scotland, both he and his wife, Janet, were born in Scotland, and they had nine children who lived in a tiny two-bedroom cottage on Powerscourt Mountain. Only the remains of the house stand among the heather on the mountain, about 100m off the road between Glencree and Sally Gap.

BIG BAG OF COMMON RED GROUSE

Irish landowners complained to Parliament that shooting parties were heading to the large estates in Scotland, Wales and England on 12 August. The Irish shooting season started on 20 August, and with the introduction of the Game Birds (Ireland) Act 1873, the start of the shooting season was changed to 12 August. The Irish record for the most red grouse shot in one day was at Sheep Banks on Powerscourt Mountain, when thirteen guns downed 358 grouse, on 25 September 1890.

SHEEP SCAB

Sheep outnumber people in County Wicklow at the ratio of 4:1. All sheep farmers fear the disease called 'sheep scab'. In 1854, a London chemist named Mr Long claimed to have found a cure for sheep scab called 'Specific', and he contacted his Irish agent, Mr William Wright of 45 Dame Street, Dublin to arrange a demonstration. The first demonstration was held on Mr Burton's farm, where there were 400 sheep on his 300 acres at Anacrevey, near Enniskerry. Mr Long examined the sheep stock, which had been neglected during the unfortunate illness of Mr Burton, who was unable personally to attend them. Several scores of sheep, which were carefully handled, were found to be in a deplorable deteriorated condition, in the lowest state of flesh and at least half their wool lost due to their leprous state. Mr Long and his assistant poured the cure on the backs of the sheep. Mr Long returned to Mr Burton's farm on 26 May 1854 and the sheep had fully recovered.

CHINESE SHEEP

In 1864, Lord Powerscourt's shepherd crossed twenty-five ewes of various breeds with a Chinese ram and produced forty-six lambs. A report of this work was recorded in the *Journal of Agriculture* in December 1865.

ROSE BRITANNIC

In 1876 The National Rose Society decided to name a rose after Richard Manliffe Barrington of Fassaroe near Bray. Richard was the primary expert in the field of ornithology in British Isles and a keen horticulturist who had cultivated a pink standard rose. Using Richard's initials, RB and his study of wildlife in the British Isles, the Rose Society decided to call the new pink rose 'Rose Britannic'.

In 1905, the Rose Society named a rose 'Revd D'ombrain' in honour of the former secretary of the society. The Revd Henry Honeywood D'Ombrain had been a curate in Bray (1841–1847), attached to St Paul's church on the Main Street.